JOURNEY TO
WHOLENESS

ALISON MARUCCHI-CHIERRO

I dedicate this book to my husband Luigi.

He has believed in me and supported me and prayed for me throughout this project. His conviction that this book is a commission from our Father God has never wavered.

FORWARD

I believe the point of writing this story of my life is to bring glory to Father God to try and demonstrate how magnificent He is and mighty to save us in all our weakness and brokenness. If just one person is helped to find Jesus and come to know His amazing love it will be a job well done.

I want to bless all those who read these words, that it will help you to develop in your own journey to

wholeness. I hope that it will not only help you to be healed of your own brokenness, but also move you to reach your full potential in Jesus. May you come to know that your Father God uniquely created you. He has a plan for your life.

In His Service,

Alison

Index

THE EARLY YEARS

The beginning of life as we count it is that moment of birth! By its very nature a dramatic event, I imagine that the angels are on special duty, the parents waiting is now over, and the joy of new life here at last. This is the ideal. Sadly, it is sometimes not so idyllic, and the expected child not always longed for, the parents not always so overjoyed.

Every birth revealing how Father God loves us, planned for us, and even delighted over us, despite the circumstances here on planet earth. We live in a broken world; the Bible tells us that when sin entered the world the world was broken. The people of the world were born into sin and were somehow intrinsically broken inside. The breaking happened when we decided to defy God. Disobedience caused a separation between all of humanity and our Father God.

We chose to deliberately go our own way. Thankfully our Heavenly Father did not leave us in this state of brokenness but made a way for us to come back to Him and the wholeness that He intended for us. This is my story, how He pursued me, and I surrendered my life, and I began to journey with Him.

My own birth took place in the country of Rhodesia, in a very small village called Rusape. My father told me the story of my arrival many times whilst I was growing up. There was great drama as they journeyed down the narrow strip road to Rusape. Mom in heavy labour urging him onwards, the old car struggling to keep going as the road had many inclines and steep descents. My mother gave birth to me only minutes after they arrived at the small cottage hospital. And to everyone's amazement I was a girl. Three boys had been born prior to my arrival and my parents were so amazed they were unable to agree on a name until I was about six weeks old. They finally agreed on Alison, a popular Scottish name with German roots meaning gift from God.

So here I was, a little girl growing up with my three older brothers. Only six years between my oldest brother and myself. Our parents kept strict boundaries for all four. We were like a unit moving together. With the close arrival of each of us we followed each other in quick succession.

Babies and then toddlers together, one after the other going off to school, High School and finally left home all in the same year. We were a family of six my mother was a stay-at-home mom, while my father worked in construction, he often had to work away from home. No matter where he was working, he always ensured that we had stability. He would never move the family to follow his job and he never interrupted our schooling.

Dad was a family man, and to enable him to provide regular family holidays he bought a caravan so that he could take us on holidays that would have otherwise been unaffordable. He also introduced us to water sports as we became teenagers and eventually sailing became a family pursuit.

Not all my memories of our caravan were happy ones, I remember one holiday when we're caravanning at a place called Kyle Dam situated near the Zimbabwe Ruins. On this occasion my parents had invited another family to join us, the children were all to be accommodated in the side tent attached to the caravan while the parents slept inside the caravan. We all had our little camp beds with a blanket and a pillow. There was a gap situated between the ground and the underside of the caravan where the wheels were.

Somehow the canvas cover designed to close this gap had not been attached. So, this resulted in a cold wind blowing throughout the night through this gap. I must have been very young, as I had not yet started school. I can still remember that cold night, I tried to hide under the blanket to find some warmth. I felt abandoned, shut out in the dark and cold. It sounds like such a trivial thing, yet for a young child it had a lasting impression, a feeling that impacted me for many years of my life. Often seeing situations through the pain, like looking through a tinted glass that made things appear distorted.

On another occasion while we were living in the small town of Mutare, it happened that our parents were entertaining some visitors. The house where we were living at the time had only two bedrooms and so to accommodate the visitors, we children were billeted in the caravan that was parked to the side of the front door. I believe that I was still quite young. What I remember is waking up in the night needing the toilet, my brothers were all asleep, and I did not know what to do. I had no choice but to soil myself. The next morning while standing outside of the front door my brothers noticed an unpleasant smell and realized that it was me.

Being boys, they made fun of me until the door was opened and we were allowed inside. To this day I still remember that locked front door, waiting outside to be let in. It reinforced my feeling of being shut out and not wanted or loved.

As the youngest in the family, my care sometimes fell on my brother's shoulders, as I mentioned before, we had all started school in close succession. We went to the local Junior School by bus, my brothers were responsible to pay my bus fare and ensure I was on the bus. On this occasion I had been left behind, I was a bit of a dawdler and had not reached the bus on time. My brothers had not noticed that I was not on the bus, so I had to walk home on my own, it was a hot day, as it commonly is in Africa for most of the year. The road was long and dusty, once again forgotten and abandoned. My personality was being formed, pulled within myself, hidden away in my Pandora's box, "Keep the lid on it, don't let anyone know how lost and alone you really feel".

There is no place too small, or situation too insignificant that Father God does not know and care about. I know that when we come to Him with our shame and brokenness, He reveals what is causing it. Sometimes we need to repent of something, at other times He graciously takes the pain away and makes us whole in that area.

I share these memories because in doing so hope that you too can see for yourself how wonderful Father God is and how much He loves you and cares for you. These small things in my life made a big impact on how I saw myself and how I reacted to things later in my life. They formed part of who I believed I was. I thought that I was not wanted or loved, and I withdrew into myself, became very shy, self-conscious, and lacked confidence.

It is evident to me, as I write these events down, that the pattern was formed when I was still so young continued to impact my life until much later. Far in the future of the actual events. The time would come when I would seek healing and wholeness from my own toxic way of seeing things and viewing myself.

Our parents, like most parents, loved their children, and they spent their lives trying to give us the home life that would be good for us. Part of the process was to have a spiritual dimension to their parenting. They became Jehovah's Witnesses, this religion teaches strong family values, but has a subtle yet destructive flaw. They teach that we need to be good enough to earn our way into Heaven, however this is impossible. The Bible tells us quite clearly.

Romans 3 verse 23

"For all have sinned and fall short of the glory of God."

The Ryrie Study Bible page 1706

An even more dangerous teaching is that Jesus Christ the Son of God, was only a man. So, forgiveness and the way of the Salvation are made null and void, thus offering no hope. My mom and dad abandoned this false religion. However, I continued to believe it and tried to carry on following until my early teen years. Believing I had to be good enough somehow to earn love and acceptance.

It was about this time I became more interested in my friends, a new thing in my life, they made me feel accepted and one of the "crowd". So began the conflict within me, a deep-seated belief that I was not good enough, not wanted or loved, yet finding pleasure in the group, the parties and then of course boys.

MY TEEN YEARS

I was not really a pretty girl, quite a heavy build and plump, and not very popular with boys. At sixteen I met Peter, he was twenty-one and seemed to like me, in fact, he even pursued me. It started initially when I met him one day while we were at a local lake where we would often go as a family to enjoy water sports. He worked with my oldest brother. Peter asked me if I would write to him while he was away for his army call-up; National Service had become mandatory. I think the soldiers were lonely and to have someone writing to you was helpful to get you through difficult times.

I was extremely flattered that he was even interested in me as he was five years older than myself. He became my first love. I was extremely inexperienced with boys and imagined that he loved me in return. The relationship was carried out for a time via letters, but on his return, it progressed and before long we were having sex.

Peter was one of the lads and loved to go to the local pubs with his friends and would bring me along. I did not enjoy this, as he loved to admire the other girls around and that continued to enforce my low opinion of myself. I was very unhappy about the way I was being treated this resulted in many disagreements with him. I asked him to take me to a dance being held at the Yacht Club where we, as a family, had spent many happy times together. He said that he would take me, but on the day, he called me and said he was feeling unwell and did not want to go out, instead he had decided to remain at home and rest. I was very angry with him; I believed it was just more of his selfish treatment of me. My brothers were all going with their girlfriends and suggested that I go with them, so I did. Not long after we arrived, I discovered that Peter was already there at the dance.

My whole world fell apart. I sobbed and sobbed. He blamed it on his friends said he had really intended to stay at home that night, but they had persuaded him to go out. Deep down I knew it was a total lie, it broke my heart and at this point I made the decision to end the relationship. His betrayal of me was irreconcilable, I told him so and went home with my brothers.

He contacted me again and wanted to come around and try to resolve the situation. I agreed to see him but asked my youngest brother to remain with me all the time he was there. I knew myself too well, I did not want to change my mind and go back after his betrayal of me. I was not prepared to let him hurt me again; I had no expectation that anything would change.

The romance had only lasted a few months, but it left me devastated, and the slow realisation that my period was late began to dawn upon me. Each day I looked hoping I would see it but of course it never came. I finally had it confirmed by the Doctor; I was already eighteen weeks pregnant. I was totally numb; I could not go back, and I had no idea how I could go forward either.

My father came to my rescue, he contacted Peter and informed him that I was pregnant. Dad invited him to come around to the house. Mom and I sat on the back step I did not even see him. He made no attempt to deny that he was the father and agreed to help with the expenses that lay ahead. It was here that the shame of what I had done and the situation I found myself in began to really dawn upon me. I had to make some life changing decisions, what was I going to do?

I could leave school without graduating; then try to get a job that would provide for both of us. At that time, I still believed that I was of no value, not wanted or loved. My experience with this man only served to reinforce my rejection. I had no confidence that I would have the strength of character to be able to carry out this plan.

Should I try to get an abortion? This was illegal in Rhodesia so was not even an option. I was already eighteen weeks pregnant, and I could already feel this new life moving within me.

The last option was to go away to a place in Bulawayo called St Claire's, a sanctuary where unmarried mothers could go and find help as they waited for their babies to arrive. There I could find safety and peace to make the most immense decision of my life. There would be no pressure there, and many hours to contemplate what I would eventually do.

I made the decision; I would go to St Claire's where I would await the arrival of my baby and determine what I would do next.

Often the consequences of what we have done continue to impact us forever, and in this case my baby as well. It also followed the predictable pattern I had fallen into, cover up, and hide it away in the Pandora box. If people didn't know about the sorrow within maybe it would go away. The truth is it does not go away. You develop defensive mechanisms, I refer to these reactions as prickles and when someone touches a prickle attached to the pain within, I would react.

ST CLAIRE'S

I had completed the first term of my graduation year at High School, having to hide my growing waistline, daily going to school not telling anyone what I was going through. Feeling the baby move inside of me while studying and struggling with what was happening inside my head. My parents were supportive, but I had withdrawn into myself, I shut them out, cried many tears alone at night, tears of self-pity, self-hatred and deep regret.

The school term finally ended, I packed up, taking my schoolwork with me. My mother and I flew to Bulawayo to St Claire's, the home for unwed mothers where I would go through my pregnancy and delivery safely. It was in this place that I found the peace I so desperately needed, it suited me well. There was order to each day; the other girls were in the same position as me. I felt no shame from them and no condemnation. Daily we had chores to perform in the home, which helped to pass the time and make the home more of a home for us all. I continued with my schoolwork, and was helped with this, by a lovely lady who was a qualified schoolteacher, who worked with me and enabled me to pass my Math, I also had History and Literature to study, and this all kept me busy.

My Aunt lived with her family in Bulawayo, and there was a weekend when my eldest brother came to visit me. He together with some of my cousins took me out to a Moto-Cross event. By this time my expanding belly was making itself evident, but one of my cousins, in his kindness, pretended we were married. He took charge of me to make me feel safe outside of my chosen sanctuary. It was a lovely thing to do that really made a lasting memory of his kindness to me. I was experiencing only kindness, support, peace and quiet while I waited for the arrival of my baby. Time to think it all through, time to make the most important decision I would ever face in my life.

St Claire's had a little chapel, which I found very peaceful, where I would go and be still. It helped to calm me, slowly I began to cry less, and the depression and self-pity were pushed back. Each week a church service was held, and after a time I was asked if I would like to help with the preparation by laying out the Minister's robes in a small vestry where they were kept, as well as setting the elements for Holy Communion. So began a weekly ritual that comforted me in a very special way.

I began doing some handiwork, creating a set of tablemats for my mother, thus helping to pass the time in a positive way. The other girls and I would take walks together, as well as our daily chores that we all had to do. I was also trying to keep up with my schoolwork, and so it was in this way that I filled my days.

One day a former resident of St Claire's came to visit us all. She had brought her son with. He must have been about eighteen months old. This girl had been one of us, she had made the decision to keep her baby and there he was for all of us to see. He played and ran around as any toddler of that age does. I looked and saw for the first time, this was not 'only a baby' I was carrying, this was a child who would need much more than to just be born. I came away with a whole new perspective of the decision I was trying to make. How could I ever be able to be the mother I would need to be for this precious child that I was carrying? As I had watched this young girl with her son, I came to realise that it was not just a baby I carried but also a little person who would need so much more than I thought I could give.

It was that day that I made the decision to give my baby up for adoption. I admired this girl, but I could not be her.

I am not sure at what point I began to pray, but I did. It became my comfort and consolation, Father God was always there, and He saw me in my mess and my brokenness, and He loved me.

My mental state had improved a great deal but as the time of my delivery approached my emotions were running high. I wrote a letter to a friend; I think it captures a bit of what I was going through. So, I will take you back to that young girl by sharing with you some extracts from a letter that I wrote to Barb with whom I had kept in contact during this time. The date of the letter was 27th August 1973 only two days before my labour came on.

"I'm still waiting and nothing's happening especially as I want to be back home for school on the 13 September. Everyone including the Doctor say that I've dropped and that I shouldn't be too long but it's still very depressing waiting"

"Tomorrow is D Day or due date, but very few people come on the exact day so I could still be waiting this time next week. I sound such a misery I don't mean to, but I feel so weepy these days. When I got Ian's (my brother) letter I just cried and cried and ended up with such a headache I felt even more miserable."

"At the moment I am timing one of the girls here contractions, I wish it was me. And another girl just came in screaming and told us she has just had a show. So maybe the ball is rolling"

That night I awoke feeling wet in my bed, surely, I had not wet myself! Then I realised my waters had broken, my wait was over, and the time for our parting was upon me. I remember standing at the bottom of the stairs with my suitcase waiting for Mrs. Smith, the lady who took care of us, to take me to the Hospital.

I gave birth some hours later, a son, who weighed in at 3.8 kilograms. I tore very badly, and I bled a lot, my lifeblood draining from me. I saw him for a moment on the delivery table, and a few minutes later he was wrapped up and in the arms of a nurse. He was taken away from me. Nothing had prepared me for this. As I lay there on that delivery table while they repaired the damage, I was being given blood transfusions to restore the blood that I had lost. The physical pain was nothing compared to what was happening inside of me. It felt like he had been ripped away from me, the bleeding, and the tearing evidence of part of my soul leaving as my heart broke.

There were two girls from St Claire's who had gone into labour about the same time as me, and so we were in the maternity hospital together. They had both decided to see their babies, just one last time before signing the adoption papers. They both tried to persuade me that I should do the same thing. The staff at the hospital advised us to wait twenty-four hours. I pondered my decision and realised if I were to see him or hold him, I would not be able to go through with my decision and walk away from him.

The next day when they came to call us, I remained behind in the ward, feeling ashamed of my lack of courage, feeling this baby deserved better than I could give him.

I returned to St Claire's for a few days, then packed up my things and returned to Salisbury, as it was then called, no longer pregnant but with a deep sense of loss. This time I travelled with one of the girls I was in the hospital with, we had shared this whole experience. As we parted at the airport, neither of us realised how our paths would cross again many years later. There is nothing in our lives that God cannot use for His glory, we cannot see it at the time we are walking through it, but He is always there even when we do not acknowledge His presence.

At that point all I could feel was that I had abandoned him to the care of strangers. All I could do was pray for him. Many years later I had a conversation with my cousin Charlie; he had been living in Bulawayo during this period of my life and was working for a company who provided Computer Services. He had made friends with another technician; they had started hunting together. It was through this connection that Charlie met Billy, who sold him a Rifle. They too became friends. One day Charlie went around to visit, only to discover that Billy and his wife Laura had just received a baby boy whom they had adopted.

Charlie immediately recognised the baby as my son. Everyone had been sworn to secrecy and so he never told me. As a result of this connection, my mum was informed by her sister, that she knew where my son had been placed.

Father God watches over His children so very tenderly, I was praying and trusting Him; He was working out His plan for both of us.

RETURN TO REALITY

And so, I came back home to my family, they met me at the airport not asking any questions and I not giving any clues about my ordeal. I never saw the child's father again. On the surface, it was as though it had never happened. I was broken hearted after what I had just come through. Now it was time to pick up the threads of my life. At a deep level I was totally changed, I was even more broken on the inside. But I had discovered a lifeline whilst I was at St Claire's. It was prayer. So, as the weeks turned into months and years, it was in prayer that I carried the son I had borne. I made it through. Without this lifeline, I would never have been able to carry on.

Soon after I returned to Salisbury I had to go back to High School and prepare for the final exams I was due to write six weeks later. I passed and graduated with enough credits to enrol at the School of Nursing in Salisbury. I had chosen this course simply because I had always enjoyed studying human biology and nursing seemed like a good option. Of course, at another level Father God had His hand on me and was directing my steps. I had made such a mess; He was in the process of putting me back together. The process of becoming whole had begun.

I would like to say I had become a Christian, but this would not be true. That process took many more years before I realised how much, I needed Father God. Until then I would continue to try to do things my way.

After sitting my exams, I met another man. He seemed to like me, so we began dating, early on in our relationship one evening while we were out together. I broke down and told him all about my son and how I had given him up for adoption. I was expecting rejection, but inwardly hoped that if he could handle the truth maybe there was a chance for us. Luigi, who I later married, was very kind and really tried to help me. Tried to love me back to wholeness. Our courtship was very stormy, he just kept bumping into all my prickles. That deep core of brokenness was at the heart of all the friction.

At this point in time the country of Rhodesia was involved in a violent civil war. All the young men were being called up into the Territorial Army and Luigi was no exception. This meant a separation for us, but we wrote many letters. Now we only saw each other when he came home for his Rest and Recuperation breaks, and part of his down time would be spent with his family. Luigi, a man of wisdom, must have loved me a great deal as he had to put up with a lot from me. I was unreasonably jealous, always expecting him to cheat on me, expecting him to meet my endless emotional needs. What patience he had!

In the meantime, I was working as a student nurse. My training involved working on the wards for set periods and then times spent in the School of Nursing. During these training breaks, lectures and practical sessions were part of the curriculum. This would be followed by a return to working on the wards where we would implement our learning. As we advanced, we were given more responsibility. At last, I had found my gift, that thing that I was created to do. I loved it, the material we were learning fascinated me, and the job itself gave me a deep satisfaction and much pleasure. No longer self-absorbed, the shyness gone, I found that in helping people who were ill gave me the opportunity I needed to give back. In a way, this began the process of getting me out of my pit of self-pity and regret. Finally, after three years of training, I graduated as a Registered Nurse, able to practice, but not feeling quite confident yet to work as a Staff Nurse.

It was at this point I decided to apply for a year's course in Midwifery. I applied to Addington Hospital situated on the beach front of Durban, a coastal city in Kwazulu-Natal in South Africa. I was accepted and a new chapter began for me. The reason that I had chosen this facility was because Luigi was at the Natal University by this time, studying for an

Engineering degree. Most of our courtship had been spent separated from each other and relied on letters to keep in touch with each other. So, I was looking forward to spending time with him.

He had asked me to marry him, I accepted his proposal. We were now engaged and planning a wedding in the July of 1977.

I had an interesting situation occur whilst flying to visit Luigi prior to moving to South Africa. On this flight I was seated between a pastor's wife and a missionary lady. As we talked together it came out that I was planning a wedding and one of the ladies asked me which church we were planning to get married in. I replied that we had not really discussed this and at this point I had no denomination to which I belonged so I imagined we would get married in a non-denominational church. When asked if my fiancé had a denomination, I said that he was a Catholic. I knew Luigi was not a practicing Catholic, hence the reason I did not think he would be concerned about where we were to be married. Both ladies agreed that it made more sense for us to get married in the Catholic Church, as I did not have a denomination of my own. This conversation set me up for the next part of my journey to wholeness. There is no detail in our lives that He is not watching over, even a casual conversation with complete strangers had moved me closer to Him in a way I would never have imagined for myself.

Luigi and I found a small flat just behind Addington Hospital. It was here that we were able to begin our life together. I commenced my Midwifery training and Luigi continued with his Engineering degree. The hospital was in such a beautiful setting, every day at work whilst attending to my patients I could look out on the vast Indian Ocean. Day or night you could always hear the crashing of the waves on the sand, always revealing a new facet of its beauty. This amazing panorama had the power to draw me in, it reminded me of a Father God out there who had created it all.

My quest for God began to intensify, and I decided the best place to find Him was in a Church. So began a weekly ritual of visiting the Priest at a Church just around the corner from where we were living. He knew we were planning to be married and it was his job to prepare me to become a Catholic. This preparation consisted of meeting with the Priest once a week for several months. He spent this time with me showing me the way of salvation, he answered my questions and explained the Catholic Faith to me. This church setting was a peaceful place, reminiscent of the little chapel at St Claire's. I was learning about the One who had laid His life down for me. This same Jesus who promised to set me free from my sin and shame. The Priest suggested that Luigi and I should participate in a course, which the Church was running for couples to equip them for married life together. So, Luigi and I embarked on a journey together. Although at the time we vainly imagined we had all the answers.

In the three and a half years since I had gone through my life changing experience I had continued to search for God, I always carried the pain of it, always thinking this thing or that person could make it all better. So here I was again thinking that becoming a Catholic would change it all for me. It began the process of healing that I so desperately longed for. Just before our wedding the Priest declared that I was ready and that he would baptise me. We agreed upon a date on an evening shortly before I was due to fly back to Rhodesia for our wedding, I went to the church with a friend I had made amongst the group of Midwifery Students I was training with.

She had planned to become a nun but had not taken her Vows. Instead, she had left the Convent and went on to train as a Nurse. She was very happy to come and be a witness to my baptism. The Priest assured me all my sins would be forgiven the moment I was baptized. I so longed for this moment; to this day I still remember the peace and joy of it. As my friend and I left, I was still a bit damp on the forehead from my sprinkling, and I knew another birth had taken place. This time the angels were singing in heaven; another lost soul had come home; I was 'born again' as the Bible calls it. The third birth in my life had no big fanfare, just the joy of being forgiven!

I believed that this peace and joy would be carried on into our marriage. I would no longer carry my burden of shame and guilt. That once we were married, I would be able to walk away from my shame. But I was not healed yet; I still had a deep core of brokenness within. I walked down the aisle just a few days later in my white dress I really felt pure and spotless, expecting to live happily ever after. But this is not a fairy story; this is about real life, about real pain and real brokenness.

MOVE TO SHAMVA

Luigi and I were married in the July of 1977, beginning our new life together as man and wife. I turned twenty-one soon after we were married. This is a significant age in our culture and signifies becoming an adult. After my baptism, and as I had walked down that long aisle at the Catholic Cathedral in Salisbury, Rhodesia it was with a real expectation that this union of lives was going to be truly amazing. This scripture truly reflected my expectations.

John 5 verse 24

"Truly, truly, I say to you, he who hears My word, and believes Him who sent Me, has eternal life, and does not come into judgement, but has passed out of death into life."

The Ryrie Study Bible page 1606

Signing the register

We went away on our Honeymoon; I was so happy! Now I could really be free to live again. I was just a new-born baby in my newfound faith. I would need the milk of God's Word to sustain me and enable me to grow and develop, as a Christian.

1Peter 2 verse 2

"Like new-born babes, long for the word, that by it you may grow in respect to salvation."

The Ryrie Study Bible page1866.

As a baby is unable to tolerate solid food for some months, I too needed to learn the simple truths about my new faith in Jesus Christ.

So, it was painful to discover my prickles were still there. My sin was forgiven, but I still carried the guilt and shame. I had not discovered the truth of our Lord's Prayer:

Matthew 6 verses 12 and 14

"And forgive us our debts, as we also have forgiven our debtors."

Verse 14 "For if you forgive men for their transgressions, your heavenly Father will also forgive you".

The Ryrie Study Bible page 1454.

I had not yet forgiven myself, and true to form I began to fix it myself. I thought it must be true; we need to perform good works in order to keep that amazing freedom real and alive. Deep within me that brokenness remained, I covered it up with my mask, but God continued what He had begun in me to redeem me.

I decided to be the best Catholic I could be, I went to Mass regularly, prayed the Rosary and believed God would intervene for Luigi and enable him to pass his year-end exams. I thought with my much praying and attendance at Mass I could somehow persuade God to do what I was petitioning Him for. This is treating God as if He is at our beck and call and expecting Him to do whatever we want Him to do. As if the sovereign God, the Creator of the Universe is there to do our bidding. That we are not trusting Him with our lives, imagining that we know better than He does. Luigi passed all his exams except for Physics. Now this is one of the major courses and could not be carried over into the next year, a huge blow for us. We had to pack up our lives in Durban and move back to Rhodesia, as it was still known at that time.

I had been able to complete my Midwifery course and had graduated. Pretty soon after arriving back in Rhodesia I started working as a newly qualified Nurse. I worked in a Catholic hospital for a time while Luigi went out to his family in Shamva to prepare a place for us to live and work. Luigi's father was farming in this area and decided to buy a farm that was near to the one he already owned. The plan was that Luigi would run the second farm for his father. I was to become a farmer's wife. Luigi had grown up on the farm and took to the move like a duck to water. He loved the farming life, spoke the native language fluently which enabled him to manage his labour force well. He deeply enjoyed seeing his crops grow and the results of his labours. I on the other hand had grown up in the city and did not think living in rural Africa amid a brutal civil war, to be on my agenda of things I wanted to be doing. I had no skills to cope with this new life.

To highlight the danger of this move; the farm that my father-in-law had bought, only became available when its owner had been killed as a result of this war! We were moving into a very dangerous situation; our first experience of this danger was when our close neighbour was kidnaped and killed soon after we arrived.

I was able to take a job as the Nurse-in-charge at Madziwa Mine Clinic where I found myself way out of my depth. The mine was situated about five miles away from the farm where we were now living, and I had to travel along a dirt road where land mines could be lurking or an ambush waiting to attack you at any point. I travelled this road twice a day, five days a week. For my protection Luigi arranged for an armed guard to travel with me carrying a fully loaded, ready-to-fire automatic weapon. Each day was a fear filled process, going to work wondering if we would arrive safely. Then the return journey, imagining what I might find when I reached home. As the only medical professional for miles around, I would be called out to attend to gunshot wounds, and on one occasion I had to attend to a landmine incident that was miles away in a remote area with only a dirt road access.

The work itself was also a big challenge for me as I worked on my own with the nearest doctor twenty miles away, accessible by telephone if the phones were working. My daily duties involved seeing to the people who attended the clinic mostly for minor ailment such as coughs and colds. Then there were the many small underground mine injuries, with the occasional serious one. The doctor who I worked under came out to the mine once a week and would attend to the problems that I might have. The doctor was also responsible to decide on work related issues such as sick notes, as well as injuries sustained whilst at work. These injuries were covered by Workman's Compensation and had to be attended to by the Doctor. Daily an Ambulance went to the nearest town called Bindura, so I could send my patients through if I decided it was necessary, a real comfort to have this facility. My nursing skills had to develop, and I was so glad I had undertaken to do my Midwifery as it had matured me as a person and given me vital diagnostic abilities that are not really taught with the basic nursing training.

What effect did all this pressure have on me? I became increasingly fearful and unhappy, I blamed Luigi for bringing me to this situation, and we began to fight a lot. By the end of our first year of marriage I was ready to walk out. I made every excuse in the world to go into Harare and stay with my parents just to get away from it all. On one of these occasions my brother took me out to a local pub for a drink and just to talk with me. I spent the evening unburdening all my issues to him. He listened patiently and agreed with me that the only solution was to divorce Luigi and get away from it all. I went back to Shamva the next day with a heavy heart, turning it over in my mind during that hour-and-a-half journey. I realized that I loved Luigi and that I did not really want to leave him, but something had to change.

I could not carry on the way I had been going. So, it was in this desperate state, unhappy but with no solution that I could see. I wondered into the mine library hoping to find a book to take my mind off it all. There I found a book called 'The Late Great Planet Earth' authored by a man called Hal Lindsey. Now this book was not new to me, some years previously, when I was still a student nurse on night duty, a patient had loaned it to me to read after we had a conversation. Anyone who has done night duty can tell you it is impossible to read on night duty, as it will put you to sleep. I had tried to read it when I was off duty, I was hoping it would help me go to sleep. Consequently, I only managed to read a small portion before returning it sometime later. I assured this gentleman, that I had enjoyed reading it.

There was the book again, "The Late Great Planet Earth: by Hal Lindsey" beckoning to me to read it. So, I checked the book out and began to read it. This time it did not put me to sleep. On the contrary, I could not put it down. Perhaps that man who had tried to introduce it to me all those years previously, had prayed for me? I may never know. The book is about end-time prophecy and through its pages I felt my heart being drawn in, right up to the final pages where Hal explains the way of salvation, a simple way to pray and receive forgiveness.

When our hearts are longing for God, He meets us on the way. For the second time I gave my life over into His hands, and for the second time it felt good to be forgiven. Yet this time it was a bit different, and I felt like I needed to do more than just kneel next to our bed and ask for His forgiveness and declare Him as my Saviour. Soon after this experience I had another opportunity to go into Salisbury. This time it was the Easter weekend, on the Sunday my parents were preparing to go to their Pentecostal Church Service. To their amazement I asked if I could go with them. That night before the whole congregation I stood up and went forward to give my life over to the One who had been with me all the time. He took me in with open arms. This time I knew for sure I was really changed there would be no going back for me. I went home to Luigi a different person.

New life in Christ

My hunger for the Bible was insatiable. I had been advised to start my reading in the book of John, but I chose to begin in the book of Matthew because it was the first book in the New Testament, and by nature it seemed right to me to start at the beginning. I just kept on going, reading at every opportunity. Finding my old friend prayer came easily, I decided to write to the thirty-plus families in our phone directory that I would be praying for them. Diligently I took the phone book out each day and just prayed through their names.

As I read the Bible, I realised many of the difficulties Luigi and I were having were a direct result of my stubborn will, that I began to rein in. I began to submit to Luigi as I learned from His Word. I became less argumentative and rebellious. Luigi was not yet a believer, that would come many years later, but our lives together began to improve.

I also began to pray about the situations I was facing at work, and I found wisdom that would enable me to perform my daily tasks. I even wrote an article in the monthly news magazine about how I submitted each day to God in prayer, and how Father God helped me in every area with which I was involved. My life was being totally turned around by Father God, thus the real process of my life-long journey to wholeness. The beginning was so dramatic, and such a change I felt that nothing could make me unhappy again. The reality is that the working out of all those things, hidden deep down inside of us, takes a lifetime of walking with our Lord and Saviour Jesus Christ.

Not long after I wrote the article in the local news magazine a local farmer's wife invited me to join the Bible Study held at her home. I was able to plan a way to be off duty and attend the Bible Study and started to join with other believers in the study of God's word. Our Topic was "The prayers of a righteous man availed much". So, my old friend Prayer began to grow in depth as some of the essential tenants of our faith were explained to me.

The deepest longing of my heart was to have another child. When a woman has a baby, her maternal instinct is awakened. Mine had been thwarted when I gave my son away. So, with every fibre of my being, I wanted to have another baby to fill this great void within me. I prayed and waited, and then I spoke to Luigi about starting a family together. We had frequently spoken of having a child, before my dedication to the Lord, but as it regularly caused contention between us, I had stopped asking. This time was somehow different, and Luigi fell silent. When I asked him what was going on, he said, "I am thinking about it". For me, this was the first glimmer of hope that he would say Yes. Then he began to discuss the pros and cons. We were still amid a war situation. Could we cope financially without my pay-cheque? I waited, telling myself "Do not coerce him, Alison! Let him make the decisions". Finally, he said yes. I was stunned. He had actually said Yes! Father God had answered the deepest longing of my heart.

It was not very long before I became pregnant with our first baby. I gave birth to a baby boy, alone again for the second time, this time at peace. The bush war was over and on the day of Giancarlo's birth, Rhodesia ceased to be, and Zimbabwe was born. Luigi had remained on the farm. He had feared that there could be trouble and felt that his presence was needed there. The arrival of this son had a bitter sweetness to it. I was so happy at last to be holding my baby, yet I could not help remembering the child I had given up. Where was he? Was he safe? Was he being taken care of? When I finally held Giancarlo in my arms the joy of it was amazing. Here at last was a son to comfort me. At last, I could release this love I had hidden and suppressed for so long.

My pursuit of the Word of God continued and one day as I was reading about a woman in the Bible called Hannah, I knew I was hearing from God. This woman was barren, a great shame in her life, she prayed to God for a child. She even bargained with God, saying that if He would give her a son, she would give the child back to Him. Her prayer was answered, and she had a son. She called the boy Samuel, which means 'God hears'.

After the boy was weaned, Hannah took him up to the Temple and left Samuel in the care of the High Priest. Samuel served in the Temple and grew up to be a mighty Judge of Israel who drew the people back to God and away from their idolatry. The story really spoke to my heart and so, on my knees, I laid my beloved son on the altar to entrust him into Gods Hands, acknowledging that Giancarlo did not belong to me, but to God. I had to remind myself many times over the years;' this boy was not my own, he belongs to God!' I was also able to let go of my first son, keeping him on the alter reminded me that he belonged to God, and I knew Father God would take infinite care of him. At times when I found myself grieving over giving him up, I would pray for him and be able to trust Father God's perfect plans for him.

It was the same with Giancarlo. Whenever I needed to entrust him to the care of someone else, I would remind myself that I entrusted him into his Heavenly Father's care. To most people it may seem a bit ridiculous to feel so over-protective, and I believe I was, but I was unable to get away from it. I had given up my first son; to lose the second one was unthinkable.

I was learning and growing in my faith, some of my layers were coming off, but deep inside I still carried my dark secret locked away, no one must know.

MOVE TO BANKET

The civil war in Rhodesia finally came to an end in 1980, Independence was granted. Rhodesia died, and Zimbabwe was born. For us this did not signal good things. Farming became impossible due to lawlessness and theft. The food crops were not safe in the fields and would be stolen overnight. Luigi would find a herd of cattle in the fields of maize, sent in by their herdsmen to graze and destroy the growing crops.

Luigi's parents had left the area the previous year because of the war, it had become even more dangerous. We had remained behind being one of only two farmers in the area. Luigi's parents had chosen to move to an area situated near a small village called Banket. Luigi's father found a farm for us to lease, close to the farm where they now lived. This would mean we could become independent and work towards owning our own farm. This new area had not suffered the same intensity of the bush

47

war. It had remained well populated. The soils were good; it was a rich farming area.

This era also signalled the departure of many of Zimbabwe's white people. By the end of 1980 my own parents, brothers, aunts, uncles, and cousins had all left Zimbabwe. Unknown to me my son's adopted family had also left the country during this time of mass evacuation. They had chosen to move to South Africa and had settled in Natal where Luigi and I had lived when we were first married.

With so much change and so many emotions, the separation from my side of the family proved to be very difficult for me. I became very discontented. I wanted to follow my family, while my husband wanted to remain near to his family. Italian family ties are very strong, and farmers are deeply rooted in the land. So, we remained.

I sustained myself in the Word of God, I knew it was my role to submit to my husband, but I did it without joy. I prayed much that Luigi would 'see the light' and realise we needed to leave Zimbabwe as well. Once again, I was trying to manipulate God who is sovereign. He knows so much better than we do and continues to work out His plan, even when we don't necessarily like what He is doing. Gradually the ship of my heart began to turn, I came to accept that we needed to remain in Zimbabwe.

I began to work again having stopped after Giancarlo was born. This time it was by taking in children. The local junior school had a boarding hostel as most parents lived too far away to commute to the school each day. The policy was that only children seven years or older were allowed into the hostel. As children in Zimbabwe started school in the year, they turned six this created a problem. Parents could either keep their children back, or home school them. The local school proposed a third option, and that was to private board the children with local families who lived near enough to the school to commute the children to school. This plan would support these children in a family environment. In the January of 1982 after our move to Banket, we took in five extra children who became our extended family. I would pick the children up from the local school on Monday at midday. Then on the Friday their parents would collect their children from the school. During the week our lives became very hectic. I would be on the road a lot commuting the children to and from the Banket School. Days were spent preparing and providing meals. Supervising and helping them with their homework. Giancarlo adapted well to all the extra children, and we had some lovely family times with these precious little ones entrusted to my care.

It was my very special privilege to pray with these children, we would sing in the evenings and read stories, and of course Bible stories as well. We did not own a television and so entertainment was very simple.

I believed I had a special ministry to love these dear ones as my own while they were in my care. To this day I am still in touch with some of these children that I took care of all those years ago.

It was during this year that we planned for another baby of our own. My pregnancy proved to be more difficult than my first two had been. With all my rushing around I had become exhausted and fell prey to any bug that was around. Having all these children about I was constantly fighting a cold, or diarrhoea, and suffered the morning sickness for most of the nine months. By the end of the year, when our baby was due, I could barely keep going. Probably as a result of this Daniela was born a week early, to our delight we had a girl! This time Luigi was around and was able to take me to the Hospital himself. From the very beginning she was a contented baby, Daniela and Giancarlo soon became the best of friends. We had our 'pigeon pair' what could be sweeter?

Sadly, because I was so very exhausted, I drifted away from Father God, and old problems surfaced. But God is ever faithful to direct our steps; He never leaves us even when we neglect Him for whatever reason. Luigi and I made the decision not to take in children the following year. In doing so we made ourselves available for the next era in this amazing walk of faith. As my health had suffered with all the extra work, I accepted that I needed to stop, I now had a young baby to take care of.

Sometime later I was contacted by another farmer's wife who lived in the district. Her name was Mary, and she was indeed an amazing nurse! She had managed a farm clinic that provided primary health care for the local farm labourers. This basically involved patients who needed medical attention such as coughs and colds, minor wounds and infections that could be treated as outpatients. The work was very similar to what I had been involved in when we were first married. Mary asked me if I would like to buy the equipment as she had decided to retire. She wanted to see her life work continued and had heard that I was a nurse. Mary thought I might be interested in her proposition. At the time we had no money to buy the equipment, but Mary brushed our concerns aside and said we could pay her as the work became established. An appointment was arranged, and I went over to their farm to collect all the equipment. Everything I would need to set up and run a Primary Health Care Clinic was there. It was that simple, and Nyahondu Clinic was born.

Giancarlo was already spending most of his days with his father around the farm. The hardest part for me was to leave my precious baby girl with a nanny, while I attended the many patients who came my way. Forgetting my previous lessons, I once again fell into my old way of solving a problem. I hated to leave my little girl, but I did not apply the principles that I had been learning about keeping my children ever before my Father and trusting Him to show me the solution.

Instead, I shut up my feelings in my box. This wrong choice resulted in many years of not understanding why my little girl showed all the signs of feeling rejected. I knew how much I loved her, yet time and again all my efforts to reach her and love her failed. I was trying to mend the problem by my good works, so why could she not see my love for her? It was many years later, through prayer, that I saw my sin of hard heartedness and by repenting and asking Father God to take my stony heart and give me a heart of flesh, graciously Father God restored my heart of flesh. The human condition! Why did I wait so long? I think it is because I was blindsided to my sin and tried instead to fix it myself. I only needed to cast this whole issue upon my Father God and trust Him to show me the better way. Wholeness had come, but all the years of heartache could have been avoided, had I not been so stubborn.

I run ahead of myself; the clinic was an amazing walk of faith. It was never my idea or my handiwork, and from the outset it was God's plan. Initially I set up the Clinic in a tin hut while Luigi got on with the work of building me a permanent structure from which to work. This building was situated near to our homestead. It was constructed with farm bricks and had a thatched roof. There were two main rooms, both of which were divided into two sections, by a wall with an entrance in it. On the one side I used to receive patients who were there with primary health care needs, using the second cubicle as an examination room affording the patients some privacy. The people who came to me had primary healthcare needs, such as minor ailments that required medical treatment. On the other side of the building was a ward with four beds, leading into a delivery room and shower cubicle. Along the front of the building was a long-covered veranda where patients came to be registered and could wait to be attended to. We were living in the tropics and the weather is hot and dry for most of the year. The clinic had been built in an area surrounded by tree's; this whole area provided a lovely cool place for the people to sit while they waited to be seen.

I registered the clinic with the local authority, and I worked under the supervision of a local doctor who attended the clinic once a week and was available to assist me if I ran into problems. The local cottage hospital would also send an ambulance if I called for one. From the very first day I opened my doors, till the last day when the clinic was closed people came to me from far and wide. I did not advertise in any way. The people found me. This was rural Africa, no newspaper to advertise, no TV, no internet. Just word of mouth and, of course God. They walked or came on bicycles with young children strapped to their backs, even using the local informal taxi service, in other words anyone with a car. It never ceased to amaze me how they came from such distances, and every day when I opened my doors they were there, waiting for me.

As with all my enterprises, I believed it was a ministry from Father God. I always prayed and believed He would direct my steps. Consequently, I employed two Red Cross trained care assistants who helped me daily. Learning a language had always been very difficult for me. The native language, Shona, was no exception. To prevent any errors arising from not fully understanding my patient's complaints one of the ladies I employed would always be at my side and translate into English so I could understand what their complaint was. She would also ensure that each patient fully understood how to use the treatment I had prescribed for his or her ailment.

The second lady would meet the patients and would record their details, issuing them with a small reference card to bring with them on their next visit. This was to enable us to find their previous card and begin to gather a bit of history to help me to make a better assessment if they should return. They would often loose the little cards. Sometimes their card could be found without it but, if not, a new one would be issued. By the time the Clinic closed some three years later I literally had crates and crates of these history cards, just to remind me of the many hundreds of people I had served through this work. In an effort to reach all the people who attended the clinic, I had a cassette recorder, playing Christian songs sung in the vernacular, and Christian books in the Shona language as well as Bibles. These were all sold at cost, to ensure that they were affordable, thus ensuring the recipient of the materials was really interested. This service also made them available for people living in an area where these materials were not readily available.

In addition to seeing the sick people I also used my Midwifery training. I would register the pregnant ladies and to try and encourage them to come for their regular pre-natal checks. I charged a reduced fee to encourage them to attend the clinic through their pregnancy. If a mother simply arrived in labour, I charged a little more as a sort of incentive for others to sign up for pre-natal care. This idea seemed to be a good one and enabled me to issue iron supplements, and generally ensure all was progressing as it should. In total I delivered thirty babies alive and well, and only had to transfer one lady via ambulance for an emergency Caesarean, this baby was also delivered alive and well.

Whatever their reason for coming to the Clinic, they were all charged a small fee, and I would dispense their treatment as part of the service. There was no chemist nearby for them to go to. Because my patients came from very poor communities, they could not afford to pay any more. If necessary, I would refer them to the Doctor who would come to the clinic once a week to see these referrals. Some would need to come back for further treatment such as dressings to wounds or a course of antibiotic injections. These patients would pay a nominal amount just to cover my cost. In all it proved to be a very good service to the community, as well as giving me an opportunity to reach out to many people with the Gospel. The money always worked out; I would have enough to pay my staff, buy the medicines and bandages I needed, and it kept food on our table for our growing family.

This work carried on for three years, while we were travelling home from a Holiday in South Africa, I felt that God was telling me that I was going home and would be closing the Clinic. Sure enough, after we arrived home, the Doctor with whom I had been working phoned to tell me that he was leaving Zimbabwe and would be closing his Satellite Clinic's, one of which was mine. So, I began the process of telling the people I had been serving that the Clinic would close on a specific day. The designated day arrived, and the flow of people stopped. From the house I looked out of my window expecting to see the usual crowd of people gathering, but there was not one. It was like a tap that Father God simply turned off. To me a real tangible sign that I had heard from Father God and that the whole project was totally His plan.

Sometimes we do not see the results of our labour in this life. I hope to meet some people in Heaven who had been helped to faith through this simple ministry.

WHAT NEXT?

Our walk with the Lord was continuing to grow. During this period of our lives, we had been attending a weekly Bible Study Group. It was through this group that Luigi had come to faith in Jesus. We had been involved in an outreach in a nearby town. One evening, we were separated into different groups, so I knew nothing of his decision until the journey home that night. He simply said, "Something happened, I am different" Indeed his walk with the Lord was always very simple and very deep. From the very beginning he seemed to just walk his faith out, without all the struggles I seemed to have.

A Presbyterian minister had started our Bible Study group, and had arranged for two other ministers, one a Baptist missionary, and the other a local Anglican Vicar, to lead alongside him. We never really felt any need to be labelled with a denomination. The teaching was straight from the Bible, and we experienced a wonderful fellowship with the group. We also attended the local Interdenominational Church in the village of Banket where each week the service was led by one of the three denominations that were leading our Bible Study group. In addition to this Luigi and I were still going to the Catholic Service once a month. In this rural setting the denomination lines became very blurred, our faith was growing, and we were hungry for more of God. So out of this need was born a monthly Fellowship Day. This would take place after the Baptist Service. As time went on two out of the three ministers had to move on. This left us with only the Baptist Missionary, who was under huge pressure from Internal Affairs who refused to renew his Visa. He was forced to return to the USA, but the group continued to meet.

After closing the clinic, we were once again taking in children to allow them to attend the local school. This time I had only taken in three children, one of whom had a medical problem that needed my skills. I was now pregnant with our third child; Giancarlo was attending the local school that year and Daniela was in her pre-school year, a busy time indeed.

Whilst carrying this baby we were going through a time of major difficulties. We were in the grip of the 1986/87 drought; it was literally months of scorching heat and no rain. Luigi was stretched to his limit. There was nothing he could do as he watched his crops fail and his cattle suffer. We prayed for rain, but the blue skies and tremendous heat continued.

Luigi loved his farm, but as the season progressed it became clear we would lose most of the crop. This meant we would not be able to repay our bank loan that we had taken out to cover the huge cost of growing a tobacco crop and running the farm. Under this extreme pressure, Luigi withdrew into himself believing that as the man he must shoulder the problems alone. True to character, I experienced his withdrawal as a personal rejection. Closed off to one another we were in big trouble. We even spoke that terrible word 'Divorce'.

It was during this very low time that I began to wish that we had not started the pregnancy. From my midwifery training a baby in-Utero can feel rejection and will be born already feeling unwanted. I was desperate for this not to happen, so I began something new for me. I began to talk with my unborn child, telling her how much I wanted and loved her. Of course, in the beginning I was doing it in the hope that Father God would undertake for my baby, but as time went on, I realised it was true. I really did love this baby who was coming into our lives. I also discovered these verses from the Bible.

Psalm 139 verses 13-16

" For Thou didst form my inward parts.

Thou didst weave me in my mother's womb.

14 I will give thanks to thee, for I am fearfully and wonderfully made.

Wonderful are Thy Works,

And my soul knows it very well

15 my frame was not hidden from Thee When I was made in secret,

And skilfully wrought in the depths of the earth. 16 Thine eyes have seen my unformed substance. And in Thy book, they were all written,

The days that were ordained for me, When as yet there was not one of them."

The Ryrie Study Bible page 928

I prayed these words over the baby who was on her way into our world. I found my faith growing and a peace coming that no matter what was up ahead, Father God held the keys to all our tomorrows. When our baby was born, she was beautiful, and grew up to be of strong character from a very early age. We named her Lucia, it means Bringer of Light, and so her arrival was welcomed instead of what might have been if I had not chosen to seek help from Father God in my time of distress.

Our Church situation, which had been great during the early days of our faith, did not help us in this time of trial. We were floating between the four church denominations, not really belonging to any of them. After the departure of the original leaders, we found ourselves without the support we needed. The Fellowship Group, as we had come to call it, were facing similar problems and other members were also feeling the strain. What could we do about it all?

We began to want more, and from this desire for more of God, a prayer meeting began. We spent time together waiting upon God, trying to discern what He wanted us to do. To help us with this, a mature couple from Harare (formerly Salisbury) would come out to the group on a Sunday for the day. We would meet in one of our homes to wait upon the Lord.

The meeting would open with a time of worship, then we would wait in stillness and quiet to hear from the Lord. This was a totally new way for us all and, when our leader decided it was time, we would all share together and test what we felt we had received during the time of waiting. The leader would write it all down for us and then pull it all together. Slowly a picture began to emerge as we met together in this way week after week. We believed we were being called to plant a church in the village of Banket, and that it was time for us to call a pastor to head up the work.

To give you a flavour of these weekly prayer meetings, I will tell you of a certain time we came together for this meeting of prayer and waiting upon the Lord. It so happened that, on this particular week the meeting was being held at our farmhouse. For some weeks prior to this meeting there had been a problem on our farm. A certain house in the workers' compound was experiencing some demonic manifestations. At night there would be knocking and other strange noises coming from the thatched roof. People reported that at night, flames could be seen on the thatch roof, but the fire did not consume it. Luigi had started taking a Bible Study in this worker's house, so Luigi had the whole labour force watching to see how he would handle the situation.

When our Fellowship Group met that Sunday, Luigi explained what was happening. Our leader said that we needed to devote some of our time together to seek direction for this problem. We had all fasted in preparation, and our meeting included a very lively time of waiting and praying that day.

The following Monday afternoon while Luigi was up on a ladder fitting a light to the house in question, he saw a small bundle of twigs tied together with string. He reached for it and pulled it out, to the amazement of those watching him. They all ran back in fear as they knew exactly what it was. The

Shona word for it is 'mushonga', which means 'medicine'. The Witch Doctors use these bundles of twigs to bind a spell to a place or a person. Luigi had been shown where the bundle was hidden. He proceeded to remove the bundle and burnt it for all to see. After this there were no further nightly disturbances and the people watching all declared that "Only your God could have shown you that". Our hopes soared, maybe now the drought would break.

There is a truth that we were not aware of. That not everything we were hearing was pure. We wanted to have continuity, but our motives were not free of our own agendas. However, I do believe what followed was of God, because we wanted everything that Father God had for us, we ran forth like teenagers to make our vision happen.

1 Corinthians chapter 13 verse 12.

"For now, we see in a mirror dimly, but then face to face; now I know in part, but then I shall know fully just as I also have been fully known. "

The Ryrie Study Bible page 1745

This walk with Father God is an ongoing surrender of our lives to Him and His plan for us. So, it was after some months of praying and waiting we finally came to a place of agreement. We had received ministry from a South African itinerant preacher on several occasions while he had been travelling and preaching in Zimbabwe. He was divinely anointed, he moved in the spiritual gifts of Revelation, Prophecy and Healing.

As a group we had not been exposed to words of wisdom and encounters with the Holy Spirit. We had not experienced anything like this from any of the team who had been leading us. It was to this man we believed we were being led to come and plant a Church in Banket. We were all hugely excited by this prospect. The imparting of a vision is a very special time and so it had been for us. But the reality of working it out can be far more difficult than we would ever imagine.

DEATH OF OUR DREAM

The drought had never let up, the crop now harvested was pitiful, our herd of cattle were weak from hunger, and we were unable to pay off our huge loan. Luigi's father, Caesar, had a house that he owned in Harare, he had kindly put his house up for collateral to enable us to qualify for our loan. Caesar could lose this property if we defaulted, a decision had to be made.

Luigi believed that he if he leased out the farm, it would enable us to pay the outstanding amount of the loan. If we could do this, we would then be able to return to our beloved farm. We would not have to go bankrupt. So, in due course, together with our little family, we moved off the farm. The cattle were herded across to my father-in-law's farm. They were so weak that some died as a result of walking just a few kilometres; the remainder regained their strength in the new environment, and their diets supplemented.

The move off the farm was chaotic; Luigi and I were still struggling in our relationship, both of us consumed by our own problems and blame shifting them over to the other one. Our household possessions were bundled up and literally dumped in an abandoned house on a neighbour's farm. We did not move into this house; Father God had other plans for us. This was an awful time of our lives. Luigi went to work for his father, as we were also indebted to him. We lived with Luigi's parents for a time and then moved into the Anglican Church Manse in Banket, this house happened to be empty at that time. It was fully furnished, so our household possessions remained where they were for a further six months. Naturally a lot of our possessions were lost or broken as a result, but I learned to hold these things loosely and to cling fast to the hand of my Saviour. We were learning a hard lesson; without God you can do nothing; that Father God wants first place in our hearts and lives.

One day just prior to moving off the farm as I was praying, I heard stronger than ever before, the voice of God. Most of my leading before this instance had been while reading the Bible, of just a gentle impression within me. This time it was so strong and clear I could not doubt it at all. The Lord said that we were to move to another farm that belonged to a couple from the original Fellowship Group.

The couple had been estranged from us when we believed we were to call a pastor, as they believed we should join up with the local church in the nearby town of Chinhoyi instead. So, I was amazed by what I was hearing. In fact, I had been praying for this couple when Father God spoke to me. The word I had heard came to pass, six months later, when it was time for us to move out of the Manse. We moved into a small two bedroomed cottage on the very farm that Father God had spoken to me about. What followed was three years of reconciliation and fellowship. Only Father God would have planned it that way; He hates it when His children fight.

The cottage was on the top of a hill with beautiful views and a lovely garden but having only two bedrooms. I still had one extra child who had come with us through all the upheaval, plus our own three as Lucia had been born during this difficult time. Our dear friend allowed us to close in the built-in garage with a large window, to form a bedroom for Luigi and me. It was in this safe place that Father God began the work of healing our marriage that had taken such a battering.

After Luigi had completed his time on his father's farm, he started a vegetable business in the nearby town of Chinhoyi. He would drive out to Harare very early in the morning to collect fresh produce, and then bring it back in time for sale in the shop that day. He would return home later in the evening exhausted, so spending very little time with the children and I. Naturally when I complained he just said it was all for us and I needed to put up with it while he established his new venture.

Not really what I wanted to hear, so in time it came to a head as these things do. In the argument that followed I made a promise to Luigi: I would get up out of bed at whatever time he did, make us both a cup of coffee, then I could pray for him, and he would pray for me. This way we would be able to hear one another praying blessing over each other at the very start of our day. Thus, began a habit that not only saved our marriage, but also became the very best part of every day. It meant that we kept short accounts on any issue we may be having. Over time we began to include other people's needs into our prayer time together.

This special time of prayer together became the glue that held us together and continues to this day. At times we would open old wounds and wash them with the word of repentance and forgiveness. Thus, the Word of God brought about much healing. Slowly and surely the layers were coming off, getting down to those deep issues that rule our souls until they are properly dealt with.

This adventure in prayer also became a very practical place where I became involved with what was going on in the business and was able to pray for Luigi as he shared the everyday needs he had.

When, for example, he needed a supply of potatoes and could find none, we would pray and that day he would find a source. It was a great comfort to see Father God undertaking for us in the little areas as well as the big ones.

Running parallel to what was happening in our own lives, the vision for a church continued. The pastor and his wife believed, as we did, that they had been called by God to move to Banket and head up the new work for the Lord. The unfolding of the plan continued, and the way forward was revealed as we moved with it. Time and again we would see Father God's providing hand. A house was found for the couple to live in and was prepared for them. A venue was found for our services to be held in. The local school had in its hostel a large room that would serve very well for us to use. At last, we felt we were ready to help this family to make this huge move from South Africa to Zimbabwe.

The Pastor served under the aegis of the Apostolic Faith Mission (A.F.M.) in South Africa, and so the work would come under their umbrella. There was another A.F.M. Church in Harare, they sent elders to help with all the administration required to set up the new church in good order.

During the Easter Weekend myself and another lady from the original group, drove down to Pretoria where the couple lived. We stayed with my mother and father who were living in Johannesburg. We had travelled in a small pick-up truck with a trailer to enable us to move the Pastors personal belongings back to Zimbabwe. It had been decided that we would travel together with the Pastor and his family on our return journey.

The following day we began the job of packing up only to discover the Pastors car had a problem. So, while the car was being repaired, my friend and I drove back to Johannesburg to my parents to get rested up. Later that afternoon we returned to Pretoria, to find there had been a terrible hailstorm during our absence. Cars and buildings had been damaged; the hail was still lying-in heaps of ice on the sides of the roads. Now in Africa to see ice lying in heaps was extraordinary, what could this mean? We did not know, but we were very grateful we had not been amid it when it happened. Father God had protected us from damage and possible loss.

By the time we reached the pastor and his family it was already dark, the Pick-up and trailer were loaded up and we set out on this long journey sometime after mid-night. We eventually reached Louis Trichardt as the day was breaking, this town was about an hour's drive from the Zimbabwe border. The Pastors car was still giving trouble, so we stopped.

The Pastor had friends in this town, and we were able to go to them. Their hospitality was very much appreciated as they fed us and let us use their shower and a bed for some hours. It was decided that my friend and I should carry on with the journey as both of us needed to get back to our families. The Pastor and his family would remain in Louis Trichardt until their car was repaired and then carry on. My friend and I finally reached home at six in the evening of the following day.

It seemed we had learned yet another lesson: this was not going to be easy, but we must not give up. We had come this far by the mercy of God. We had been in the battle, not realizing how hard it would be. This was only the beginning, but it gave us renewed courage to persevere, this work was going to develop into something amazing.

It is significant that Father God wants us to grow in our relationship with Him at the outset of becoming involved with any major work of His. As a group we began to depend on Him more and more.

Proverbs chapter 3 verses 5-6

"Trust in the Lord with all your heart,

And lean not on your own understanding.

In all your ways acknowledge Him, And He will make your paths straight."

The Ryrie Study Bible page 941.

Over the next weeks and months, we grew better able to stay true to the course when we encountered the many trials as the Church in Banket was established.

As planned, the services began in the school's hostel. Our numbers dwindled, and some left to go back to the mainline denomination, while others came and added to our numbers. Our individual gifts began to emerge. My friend with whom I had travelled to Pretoria was a talented musician, Luigi became the administrator and was very involved in the accountability side of things. I began the children's work; it seemed to be the area that fitted me well. I even started taking Religious Instruction classes at the local School where we had our weekly services.

The busier I became, the less I felt that pain deep inside of me. But my sharp edges were still there and, as hard as I tried, they did not go away.

As Paul said in Romans 7 verse 19:

"For the good that I wish, I do not do; but I practice the very evil that I do not wish."

24 "Wretched man that I am! Who will set me free from the body of this death?"

The Ryrie Study Bible page 1712.

I would mess up, then repent and ask for forgiveness, but always feeling condemned, trying so hard to cover up my sin yet falling back into it time and again. I had a terribly bad temper; I was compulsively jealous over Luigi and over sensitive to everyone trying to work with me. I tried to cover my sin with a mask; the only one I was fooling was myself.

I thank God, He is so good to us, He sees us, and He knows us, and incredibly, still loves us. I was brought to a place and a specific teaching:

James 1 verses 6-8

"6 But let him ask in faith without any doubting, for the one who doubts is like the surf of the sea driven and tossed by the wind.

7 For let not that man expect that he will receive anything from the Lord,

8 being a double minded man, unstable in all his ways."

The Ryrie Study Bible page 1857.

The teaching highlighted by this scripture described me so eloquently. I was unstable; I had experienced several bouts of depression over the years. I had learnt not to indulge my imagination, as it would lead to self-pity and depression. As a result, I had given up reading fictional books. Having discovered how to give my problems to the Lord in prayer had also been a major help to me. But despite all this I was still unstable and double minded. I could not fix what was broken in me. So, led by the teaching in James, I prayed a prayer that was to change my life.

"Dearest Father God, remove from me all that is false, strip away all that is not real, and my own way of trying to fix my brokenness."

I walked away from that prayer feeling no different but having tapped into something that totally changed my life and my walk with the Lord. It began slowly, like the sands inside an hourglass, running through a tiny hole emptying into the bottom chamber.

I began to see that much of my busyness was of my own doing. I had said 'yes' to anything that was available to be done to try and please people and make myself feel indispensable. I began to lay down much of what I was involved in. I gave up the work with the children at church, thus releasing others who had better gifting and talent than I had been in this area. I realised much of what I had thought was the redemptive work of the Holy Spirit was in fact my own efforts to be free.

I began to remember things in my past that had so impacted my life. As I asked the Holy Spirit to expose it all, He did. Tears and sorrow were my daily companion. I cried for the little girl who had felt so shut out and abandoned, and God comforted me and made me whole in that area.

A major problem in our marriage was my inordinate distrust of Luigi. I expected him to be unfaithful, and so I was always looking for the evidence of his unfaithfulness. It would tear me up inside if he would pay another woman any attention. I was so miserable. As a result, Luigi would take every opportunity he could to get away from me. He would often go fishing with his friends, leaving me at home alone with the children.

Then one night in a dream I saw the root of it all; when I awoke from the dream, I could still see it in my mind vividly. It was the incident with Peter the father of my first son. He was my first love I had been only sixteen. The pain of the betrayal had cut very deep. In my mind I had made him responsible for giving up our son for adoption. I was confronted by my own choice and the decision that I had made as a result of it. So down on my knees I went and forgave this man and set him free, and in doing so I set myself free. The power of forgiveness is immense, and it brought a great healing in my life.

I was also confronted by my terrible temper. To realise how much this temper of mine had kept my children in fear of me was appalling. I saw it in all its ugliness, so I confessed my sin to my children and Luigi. They of course knew all about it, it was I who had been deceived.

I believe Luigi must have seen a change in me and felt the tug to get busy with his own issues. We went for counselling. Those sessions brought out things I knew nothing about. If I had not seen my own sin in such clarity, my reaction would have been self-righteous and judgmental. Instead, I knew the way forward was the way of forgiveness. Jesus forgave me so much, how could I not freely forgive Luigi. So, layer-by-layer the mask was being peeled off, this time Luigi and I were doing it together, our relationship was being healed. When you have exposed the worst to the one you love, and they carry on loving you it sets you free from the bondage of secrets and lies.

There was still one lie, one secret which I was keeping from my children and from everyone who knew me. That was of course the child whom I had given up, who was safe in the care of his adoptive family.

As we allow God to remove the layers that cover up our sin, we come into a deeper level of intimacy with our heavenly Father in this journey of life. It is a journey in which we learn to be real. There is a poem that really describes this process that I will share with you.

<u>The Velveteen Rabbit: Margery Williams</u>

Rainbows through Clouds, 1997 by Lady Glover

" How can I become real?"

The little Velvet Rabbit asked the old Rocking Horse.

"It's something that happens to you when someone loves you,

For a long time, really loves you." "Does it hurt?"

"Sometimes," answered the Rocking Horse,

''But when you're real you don't mind being hurt. "It doesn't happen all at once, you slowly become real"

It takes a long time, and it does not happen to people who break easily,

or have sharp edges."

"By the time you are real,

your velvet will be worn out

and loved off, and you will look really shabby, but these things don't matter at all.

Because once you are real you can't be ugly, except to people who don't know how to love?"

This process of becoming real takes a lifetime; it will not be over until that day when we meet Jesus. To this day I still have times of revelation of my heart. I can relate to the Apostle Paul who, at the end of his life, said that he considered himself the chief of sinners.

THE HARVESTER

Meanwhile the church plant was progressing. We believed that, as a group, we needed to buy a local Hotel that was in the middle of Banket Village. In its day it had been a lovely 'Colonial' hotel, but over time it had become the local place for alcohol consumption and prostitutes. The village is on the main trucking route from South Africa to the North African countries. Through demographic studies it became known that the truck drivers were spreading the HIV/AIDS virus. The hotel had become very run down and now its owner wanted to sell it.

We believed it could become a wholesome place for the community to find Jesus, where we could host various meetings as well as use it as our meeting place for the Church.

The vision for The Harvester was about to be born. The name we gave it came from our deep desire to see the facility used to harvest souls for God's Kingdom. To turn back the evil that had come to our village through this place. To bring life instead of death from the dreaded HIV/AIDS virus that had been spread so far and wide from this place. Sometimes in this life we get a tiny glimpse of the Fathers Heart to heal us all and, I believe that is what The Harvester was all about.

It all began by the joining of the hearts of five men to that of our Pastor, who was a man of vision. These men and their wives came together in prayer, believing they had a mandate from the Throne Room. They put their skills and their money into the project. Luigi was one of these men. At first, he could not put any money in, as we were still struggling to pay back the money we owed to the Bank.

Our Tenant had failed to pay the agreed contractual rent money that he had agreed upon. The result of this failure to keep to his commitment was, that our beloved Nyhondu Farm had to be sold. We laid our dream down and sold the farm to pay off our debt. Only then was Luigi able to give money into the vision of The Harvester. He did it with great joy, and he became officially a director with the other four men.

After the transfer for the hotel had taken place, we were allowed into the building. The founding men had all been in before this, but it was only now that the rest of us had been allowed inside. It was very dirty, and the smell of spilt beer and cigarettes was everywhere. The main kitchen just smelt dirty and did not seem to have been used for a while. There were all kinds of equipment, some items we were able to use, others had to be destroyed.

Our first objective was to clean up the downstairs toilet, as well as the main lounge to make it ready to hold our first Church Service on the following Sunday. I can still remember using many buckets of water and disinfectant on the toilets to make them serviceable.

On that Sunday we came together to hold a thanksgiving service in the main lounge, giving the Glory of it all to Father God. We were still a relatively small band of people but, as the renovation work got under way, we found the community delighted to join in with us. People gave their time and talents, also their money, when they saw it starting to take shape.

A certain grand, elderly gentleman of faith, together with his friend, offered to re-plant the garden that surrounded the hotel. This gentleman happened to be a leading expert on indigenous trees, and his friend was responsible for the Botanical gardens in Harare. So, it was no surprise that the garden turned out to be a place of beauty, a real oasis in our dusty little village. This same gentleman also cut down a special tree from his farm that he had nurtured for many years and fashioned it into a very beautiful cross for the 'Sanctuary' as we came to call the place of worship.

The initial work was very messy. It involved clearing out the two main bars, completely removing all the fittings and stripping the walls down to plaster. The main bar, which had its entrance coming out onto the front veranda, was to be used as the Sanctuary where we held our Worship services. The second bar, which opened out onto a walled-in- area at the back of the building, was chosen to house the children's work. This walled-in-garden also received the attention of our two grand gentlemen, and, with the addition of some playground equipment, it served the children very well.

The Sanctuary was also adorned with some beautifully crafted banners, created by very talented ladies in the church. A worship band began to form and the equipment to go with it was acquired. Much time and effort to understand about worship, and people willing to learn and develop their talents resulted in great times of worship in this place. It was amazing to see all the talent that Father God had assembled.

In these initial stages I had continued to be very involved with the children's work, I longed for the children to experience the Lord in a very real way. As I mentioned earlier, this was not the ministry that I was meant to continue. Father God had selected others for this work and so I stepped aside at the right time so they could take over the work that flourished in their hands.

My real passion and longing were always in the ministry of prayer and, as my life was slowly but surely being restored, it was to this ministry that I devoted my time. Every week, in the upstairs prayer room, I would meet with the wife of one of the five founding men. This lovely lady had organised for this room to be painted, curtained and furnished for the specific use of prayer. We were not the only ones who used it and, we were by no means alone in this ministry of prayer, but we were the two who were always there. We met each week and waited on the Lord, prayed through the various concerns that had come to us, and rejoiced to see what Father God had done.

As the work of restoration continued, our numbers were added to as people wanted to get involved with what we were doing. We began to see purpose and meaning as restoration of the building and the people continued.

In the main entrance was a magnificent staircase leading upstairs to where the rooms were situated. There was a small apartment that was re-styled into a flat big enough for a couple to live comfortably. This accommodated a young couple, who believed they had been called to join us. Their role was to care-take and establish future expansion.

Our expansion plan included transforming the cocktail bar situated in the entrance hall, into a coffee shop that would serve light meals as well as refreshments. We were hoping to host local conferences, church meetings and national conferences.

Another lady had a vision to set up and run a Christian Library that would lend out books, videos, and audiocassettes to train and equip people for ministry. To house her large collection, the office on the other side of the entrance was converted into the library. It was suitably cleaned, painted, and fitted with shelves. It was also fitted with a bay window, this displayed the materials available inside, thus enabling people coming into the entrance to see what we were all about.

Eventually the main lounge was also used for exercise classes, local Council meetings, and hospital staff training conferences. If it was wholesome and benefited the community, we welcomed them in. Even the Children's Church facility was used during the week for a Nursery school.

These were exciting times; it seemed that all was going to plan. But then there arose criticism from within, and factions began to form. Some of the people, convinced they were the only ones who knew what was right, wanted their own agendas. It finally came to a head, leading to confrontation with our beloved Pastor. He took his family and returned to South Africa.

The couple in the flat left as well. We were gutted! How could it have happened, when it all seemed to be going so well? The answer, I believe, is that we can drift off the mark in the excitement and imagine we can do it ourselves, allowing pride to creep in.

Luigi continued to hold services each Sunday. The first Sunday he preached to only us, his family. I picked up running the Coffee Shop, and we moved out of the little cottage on the hill into the house that had served as the home to our departed Pastor. We were standing in the gap, holding on. Luigi is very skilled at delegation, and he soon had arranged for local lay preachers to come and preach at the services. The Worship team came back and once again to lead the 'Praise and Worship,' so things settled into a rhythm but only for a season.

The next development was when a large Church in Harare agreed to come in and help us to recover fully from what had truly been a crushing blow. Each week they sent one of their ministers to lead the service. Over the course of time one of the ministers was chosen to move out to Banket to head up the work of The Harvester. Father God had ordained the work and He continues to use this facility to this day.

HOME SCHOOLING

As the different areas of my life were being re-aligned by Father God, a new direction began to emerge. I had, from very early on in our children's lives, wanted to home-school them. The dream had waxed and waned over the years, depending on where I had been on the pendulum, and public opinion had held a big sway in my life.

This had been the reason I had started the children's work in the church, I had always believed that it was vital to sow the Word of God into our children's lives. I had even written long term prayers for each one of them on egg shaped pieces of paper and placed them in an old Bible, symbolic of trusting God with it. For each one on the top of the list of things that I desired for them was a Christian education.

Now that Father God had cleared away the false areas in my life this passion remained. I did not have the support of anyone; I was considered just a bit "over the top" on this one. I wanted our children to be mighty men and women of God who would reach loftier heights in the Kingdom than I felt I had done, where I had messed up so badly in the beginning.

Living in the new Zimbabwe we found ourselves constantly in a crisis, the education system we had grown up with was under siege. Quite rightly, the new government wanted every child in our nation to receive a good education but to achieve their goal they were forcing many more children into classrooms than a single teacher could cope with. They practiced a system called "hot seating", which meant the seats in the classrooms had to be constantly filled. There would be one set of children using them in the morning and then a second set of children would be taught using those same seats in the afternoon. Extra-curricular activities were pressed out in the same way. Now huge numbers of children were getting to go to school, but there was very little in the way of support for your average pupil. Only the very bright ones were getting a real education. Teachers simply did not have the time to spare for the ones who may be struggling. Added to the problem was the fact that there were not enough trained teachers, so the older pupils were employed to teach the younger ones.

This led to a proliferation of Private Schools. There was a great divide between those who could afford the new schools and those who could not.

We fell at the lower end, Giancarlo and Daniela started grade 1 at the local government school we had been a part of for so many years. But by the end of Giancarlo's grade two year, we realised we would have to move them out into a Private School. The decision was made they would go to a new school in a town called Karoi. The school was too far away for me to commute, and the hostel facilities were full. I now had to entrust my precious children to a lady who was doing what I had done all those years ago. It literally broke my heart to send them away, how could this be right? But it seemed to be the only solution at this point in time.

Deep down I believed this was my Ishmael. In the Bible story about Abraham, we discover that God promised Abraham a son. The problem was that Sarah his wife was unable to conceive. This resulted in Sarah and Abraham taking matters into their own hands. Abraham slept with his wife's maid, and they produced a son whom they called Ishmael. Ishmael's arrival had resulted in much strife and heartache in the family. Finally, God enabled Sarah to conceive, and she bore Isaac the son God had promised to Abraham. But poor Ishmael and his mother were sent away. I believed that somehow my faith was too small to wait for the emergence of Gods perfect plan for our children.

I still had Lucia at home, but she was almost like an only child, as her brother and sister were away at boarding school. I hated Monday morning when they would have to go back to school, and my spirits soared on a Friday when they were due back home. How would I ever be able to stand my little five-year-old to go off to boarding school.

I devoted a good deal of my time to praying for the schooling issue, continuing to believe God was able to bring my deepest longing for Christian Education.

The time for Lucia to go to school was rapidly approaching; Giancarlo was in his final year of Junior School. We enrolled Giancarlo into a Senior School close enough for him to take the bus daily to school, no longer having to board. Lucia was to commence junior school in Karoi, joining Daniela who had already been boarding with her brother for four years. Sending my girls off to boarding school, just felt so wrong! Here was our twelve-year-old son (Giancarlo) being the day scholar, and our five-year-old baby girl (Lucia), and Daniela going away to be a border's. My heart was not in this one, but what else could I do, our children needed to be educated.

So, with a heavy heart I did what was needed for all of them. Giancarlo commenced High School in Chinhoyi,

Lucia and Daniela at Junior School in Karoi. Lucia seemed happy, she took to school life very well, no tears or tantrums, and earned the title of 'Miss Chatterbox'

Daniela continued on without her brothers support, but now became her little sister's support.

As that year progressed Luigi's mind began to change over the home-school issue and, halfway through the second term of that year we made the decision to bring the girls home, I would now home-school them both. We took Daniela and Lucia out of school at the end of that year, having made extensive preparation for them, at last I had my children home again and my vision for them was about to come to pass.

The choice of curriculum was made; we would use the Accelerated Christian Education (ACE) system that was well established in Zimbabwe. The ACE system provided training for the supervisors, as I would not actually be teaching the girls only 'supervising' their learning. There was another family who were struggling to educate their girls, so it was arranged that these two girls would join us. Their father constructed desks following the plan that we received from the ACE manual. Each desk was designed to provide space for three students working together and had removable partitions so that the children working together would not be distracted by one another. We set our classroom up in one of the rooms at The Harvester, so we could have a place separate from home that we could call school. I had also made uniforms for the girls to give them their own identity.

Daniela and Lucia were tested at the ACE centre in the town of Rusape where I had been born. From this testing it was established exactly where the girls fitted into the program. The program was everything I wanted for the girls. In addition to learning Math and English they studied the Bible and godly principles for life. Weekly we would study and memorize sections of Scripture that I would choose for them, and with each subject they would have a memory verse to learn as they worked through that study booklet. In their Literature series they Studied Christian Classics, as well as true stories of the lives of people who had done great exploits for the Lord. For me the program was so wholesome and full of the Word of God, I could not have been more delighted with it.

As I look back, I think perhaps I was overly strict, keeping to the plan very closely. Not being a trained teacher, I was not very creative in the classroom. I wanted the children to be able to absorb as much as they possibly could from the materials. I also worked very hard at giving them outside exposure to other children and extracurricular activities. They both received piano lessons from a local piano teacher, dancing lessons, as well as being allowed to join in with tennis classes held locally.

Sadly, the other family pulled out after the first year. Education is a Long-term project and a big vision of mine. I had always imagined there would be many other parents who would catch the same vision for their children. Sadly, this did not happen, so I continued with Daniela and Lucia. One family in the nearby town of Chinhoyi also started their own class, as well as another family who lived some distance away. We made plans together for end of term social activities, as well as prize giving. With these events we encouraged one another, as well as helping our children not to feel so out of step with the children who were attending regular school.

After two years of home-schooling Daniela, was now due to commence senior school. My confidence in my own ability to continue wavered. Daniela was terribly shy, and the home schooling seemed to only make the problem worse. Luigi and I prayed with each other, and then spent time praying with Daniela. Slowly between the three of us, we came to the decision that Daniela would re-join the main line schooling system. She would go to the same school where Giancarlo was already enrolled, and commute with him to school on a bus that ran daily. After two years of home schooling, the first year back in regular school was very hard for Daniela.

All the friends she had made in junior school had spent the last two years continuing at boarding school. They had enjoyed school trips together and Daniela had missed out on all of this. They remembered her, but she never really managed to re-establish the friendships in her year. Added to this problem was the fact that Daniela was born in December. She had gone to Grade 1 when she was already six years old. The result of this age difference was that Daniela was more mature than her former classmates. Her experience of home-schooling had also estranged her from her former friends due to her completely different experience. However, Daniela did make some wonderful lifelong friends with time, as it happened who were mostly her own age or older.

I continued to Home School Lucia for one more year but to keep her at home on her own was simply unkind. So, after two years with Daniela and three years with Lucia, I conceded defeat and laid it all down, Lucia was enrolled at the Junior School attached to the Senior School where Giancarlo and Daniela were at school.

When we had first conceded that we needed to put our children into a Private School. We had chosen not to put Giancarlo and Daniela into this school. The Head Teacher at that time, was creating a culture in the school that was totally unacceptable to our Christian principles. He had subsequently left and had been replaces by a godly man whom we respected. It had been for this reason all those years previously that we had chosen to send Giancarlo and Daniela to Rydings Junior School that was so much further away.

When I look back at those prayers and how I placed our children into Father God's Hands, I see how He carried them for me. Giancarlo finished school and went to a Bible College in America where he received his Christian Education. When Daniela left school, she also attended the same Bible College as Giancarlo. Lucia came back and was Home Schooled after only two years of High School. This choice was made as a result of Lucia realising, she was getting into bad company. She wanted to return to home-schooling. And so, Lucia also completed her Christian Education.

Father God was faithful in answering my prayers for our children. I just want to say that nothing is a waste in God's Kingdom. As our steps follow His steps, they will take us to where He wants us to be. Children are a blessing from the Lord, but we only have them on lone, they really belong to Him.

MOZAMBIQUE

The new Pastor at The Harvester had a vision for ministering to the surrounding nations; we had Zambia to the north of us, where several people from our farming community had relocated. The future of the white farming community in Zimbabwe was under siege, and many people had relocated for this reason. Zambia was now being rebuilt and did not seem to need our church's assistance.

Then there were our neighbours to the east of Zimbabwe, Mozambique; this nation had suffered a protracted civil war. Finally, it had come to an end, and the border to Mozambique was re-opened. It was to this very broken nation that the church leadership turned their attention and decided this needed further investigation. A trip was arranged; only the men were to go as it was considered too rough for any of the women to be included.

Luigi and Giancarlo signed up; Giancarlo must have been about seventeen at the time. They all took camping equipment with them, as well as all their provisions. It was unlikely that there would be anything available once they crossed over the border. The trip was a great success; the group returned and reported here was a nation in great need. The entire infrastructure had been destroyed by the many years of civil war; the roads had huge potholes as a result of land mines. They observed that most of the buildings needed repair; no maintenance had been done during the years of conflict. The railroads were derelict, burnt out tanks and army vehicles abandoned and rusting where they had been left.

Far worse was the state in which they found the people of Mozambique. They had very little food, and few possessions, some wearing only animal skins. The people were living in makeshift huts and the majority were unemployed. Somehow, they had survived; no wild animals could be seen as they had been hunted for food to keep people alive. Mozambique has a very long coastline and fishing had also played a major role in helping the people, it had saved many lives. There had been no agricultural activities during those many years of war; it had just been too dangerous.

The group returned home inspired to help, but what could be done for this nation? They had also visited a mission station which had continued to function throughout the war. Their mandate was to take care of the many orphans who were brought to them. There was a small school, a clinic, and the main compound where the children and people in their care lived. There was also a large building only half completed that was called The Church. It was a large structure that consisted of a roof with three sides and a dirt floor. It seemed obvious that here was a place already established and in great need of assistance.

The life in Mozambique was at such low ebb that Luigi's comment was "you would really need to be called by God to want to go to that place."

It was therefore quite incredible when this bizarre thought came to both Luigi and I quite separately. That it was us to whom God was calling. Neither of us told the other one, feeling it was just totally out of the ballpark, but then one-night Luigi shared with me what he was sensing in his spirit. I was absolutely amazed as it was exactly what I was sensing. It was electric! We became excited as the thought began to grow in us.

Luigi called our Pastor, to share what we thought we were hearing, and our Pastor became as excited as we were. After this, all the Eldership gathered, and the vision was shared with them. They agreed that this thing was from Father God. It was decided that we needed to make a second trip to the Mission Station. This time we would take our family with us before making the final decision. We made the arrangements needed for the trip; our children not fully aware of what it was all about, but always up for an adventure.

The couple that headed up the work had been at their post throughout the duration of the war. They were exhausted; they had stood firm through it all, but now needed to take some time off to rest and recuperate. During the war, the wife had been abducted and taken on a very long cross-country march by the Frelimo activists who later became the ruling government. She and some other missionaries were held hostage for many months, but finally they were all released, and she was returned to her husband. Even after this terrible ordeal she returned to the mission station and carried on as if it had not happened.

It took several years for her to truly recover from the whole episode. They wanted someone to stand in the gap to give them the freedom to be released and take the rest that they so needed. I was a trained nurse, experienced in Primary Health Care, having worked in the rural clinic setting. Luigi had been a farmer and had established his own business, so had good management skills. Together we seemed to fit the bill.

Here on earth, we can only see in part, and what seems right is not always so.

1 Corinthians 13 verses 9 and 10.

"For we know in part, and we prophesy in part: but when the perfect comes, the partial will be done away"

The Ryrie Study Bible. Page 1744

We needed to seek further council before making such a major decision, and so we returned to Zimbabwe. It was not only Luigi and I; we had three children to consider. How was it all going to fit together? There was a lot at stake; both Daniela and Giancarlo were in their senior years of High School. Giancarlo was preparing to write public exams that would be critical for his future. Daniela was not too far behind him in this regard.

We turned to the leader of the church in Harare who provided The Harvester with spiritual covering. This Pastor knew Luigi well as an elder and we trusted him. He believed it would be better for us to be sent out by his church, as the Mission Compound we were considering lacked formal covering and oversite. This Pastor persuaded us that his church would offer us the cover and protection we would need as we went out to the Mission Field.

His church had been taking care of refugees from Mozambique for several years and they were preparing to send them back home. At that point in time the church was involved in building in a placevcalled Tete`. This building project was to include a church, as well as a house for a Pastor, and some offices. Tete` is situated on the Great Zambezi River, and was much further north than we had been on our previous trip.

A godly American was facilitating building of churches all over Africa; he had identified a need that he was able to meet. The church in Tete' had been commenced by another American who had come over to supervise the building work. The supervisor had fraudulently drawn the money but had failed to complete any building. This had resulted in a lot of money being squandered and very little on the ground to show for it.

It was proposed that Luigi would take over the work, live on site and get the job done. He would be paid a salary for his work. I was to remain in Zimbabwe with the children and run Luigi's business that he had worked so hard to build up. It was settled literally in an afternoon, my head was spinning, and little did I realise what a trial I had just stepped into. Our relationship would be stretched to its limit, and it would result in a deeper healing in my journey to wholeness.

We soon settled into a routine, Luigi heading out to Mozambique early Monday mornings, and returning late on a Friday or Saturday. I would get the children onto the school bus and then head into Chinhoyi and run the business. My skills as a businessperson were limited, and this resulted in me being taken advantage of several times, due to my naivety in business. I was lonely and felt that old feeling of being left behind emerging again. Luigi on the other hand just loved it, he felt this was his purpose, his skills were being used, and he had a real determination to get this job done. It was a big adventure; he was excellent at crew management and possessed good knowledge and experience of building in Africa. His language skills were good. He spoke the vernacular and his first language, Italian, enabled him to learn Portuguese, the language of Mozambique.

My feelings of inadequacy and rejection surfaced again, I was not coping, and it all came to a head the week that Luigi was going to put the roof onto the Church. He had borrowed some lifting equipment from one of the church members and he was taking it back to Tete' that week. I was consumed with a huge sense of foreboding that morning as I went into work. I could not get myself together, so I prayed and prayed but it did not lift. I felt so isolated and alone.

That evening I called Luigi and a woman answered the phone. It was the lady to whom Luigi was accountable. She was responsible for the finances and making sure all was going to plan. When he came to the phone, I asked why he had not told me that she was going to be there? He said that she had only informed him that morning when he had called by at her house on his way to Mozambique to collect some money for the work. He was totally alone with her on site; even the Pastor, who was normally on site, was away for some reason. Luigi had not told me; he knew well that I would not have been happy for him to have put himself into this position.

The reality was that she was his boss, and true to character Luigi was single minded in his determination to get the roof onto the Church. He had the use of the lifting equipment for only one week. I asked him to come home. He said he would, but he really needed to get the roof on to the Church. He succeeded and came home on the Thursday; he had been able to get the job done quickly because of the equipment that he had borrowed.

Luigi putting the roof on.

Morning devotions with the staff.

I met Luigi and his boss at her home in Harare. I was confrontational, but we talked at length about the propriety of what she had done. The reality was that nothing had happened, and the situation demonstrated so clearly that I was not free from my insecurities, which were still very much apparent through this whole situation.

Our lead Pastor was contacted, and a meeting was convened. It consisted of Luigi, our Pastor, and the Lead Pastor, as well as me. I was told in no uncertain terms that I was not missionary calibre because he believed I did not have the strength of character that it required. Luigi was given a week off before he returned to site to complete the work.

This time I went back with him for a week. It was a very special time to be a part of what Luigi had such a passion for, I was filled with shame and feelings of failure were back to haunt me. Over the week I was comforted as I shared in all that Luigi was doing. This special time enabled me to carry on. Once again, I found my peace in trusting the whole situation into Father Gods' hands.

Luigi successfully completed all the building in time for the inauguration of the Church by the whole team of people who had been involved. The children and I were there to help him finish off well. The girls and I cleared the site of all the rubbish and polished the floor of the church. All the while Luigi and Giancarlo were working together on the final touches to the buildings.

After the church and compound had been inaugurated, we went as a family to the mission station we had visited earlier, to see how the couple were getting along. We found that, since our last visit, they had both been receiving help and support and were now both doing much better. We were also able to see them on subsequent visits in Zimbabwe and it was apparent that their needs had been met.

Luigi and I were enabled to fulfil the mandate we had received, but this time it was in Zimbabwe with another mission organisation who were looking after widows and orphans from the HIV/AIDS epidemic, but that is another story.

IN THE MEANTIME

What was happening to my first-born son over these years after my first, and only sight of him?

He was born in The Lady Rodwell Maternity Hospital in Bulawayo but had to remain in for longer than usual as he was suffering from Neonatal Jaundice. He had then been adopted by a family who lived in Bulawayo, this is where my cousin had recognised the baby as my son. Life in Zimbabwe was increasingly difficult because of the war and many families left the country. My son's family were among those. They emigrated to KwaZulu-Natal, in South Africa.

My son had an older brother, and his father was a devoted family man who was very involved with his children. He would take his sons fishing with him were they learned many skills. He did well at school and grew up surrounded by a family who loved him.

Sadly, when he was 14 years old his father was diagnosed with Lymphoma Cancer, the disease progressed until his father passed away while his sons watched on.

For any child the loss of their father, is a life changing experience. As you can imagine, it had a major effect on him. He was devastated, broken and angry, why would a good God take his father? A troubled teenager, he became reckless and fatalistic. The loss of his father hurt so deeply; he did not know how to deal with it. He began to consume alcohol to try and silence the pain. He decided there was no God and, if He existed at all, he didn't care much for Him, and did not want anything to do with Him. Trying to manage this storm of emotions in his life, he pretended that he couldn't care less; his personal life was a mess.

After he completed his high school, he was conscripted to serve his country in the South African Army. South Africa was at war with Angola, so every young man reaching the age of eighteen years old was called up for National Service. He travelled to Pretoria to undertake his mandatory training. During this time, it was compulsory for the troopers to attend a weekly church service.

As he sat in one of those church services he was still struggling with the hurt, anger and brokenness that he carried as a result of his father's untimely death. He had all his usual ammunition against God, believing that He was not a good God because He had taken his beloved father away from him. Again, he told God that he did not care for Him. The scripture being expounded at that service was the following:

Romans 8 verses 14 to 16

14; "For all who are being led by the Spirit of God, these are sons of God."

15; "For you have not received a spirit of slavery leading to fear again, but you have received a spirit of adoption as sons by which we cry out, Abba! Father!

16;" The Spirit Himself bears witness with our spirit that we are children of God."

The Ryrie Study Bible page 1713

This message kept speaking directly to him. It was as if God was talking to him directly. Little did he realise at the time that this was the Holy Spirit, the way in which God speaks to His children. Finally, my son ran out of ammunition, God demolished all his barriers, and he surrendered his life to the One who gave His all to save him. He had begun his journey to wholeness, another new birth; there was much rejoicing in heaven over a prodigal coming home.

THE WINDS OF CHANGE

We found our lives caught up in the winds of change that were blowing throughout Africa. Our lives had been dramatically changed when our son Giancarlo followed his sweetheart to America to enrol in a Christian Bible School. They were married in 2002 and any hope of them ever returning died. Daniela followed her brother to America also in 2002 and enrolled at the same Bible School that Natalie and Giancarlo attended.

To travel to America was difficult for us, our son and his wife could not travel to Zimbabwe as they had applied for political asylum. Inflation was now unbelievably high in Zimbabwe. Each day our money could buy less than the day before. Fast forward to 2006 and our youngest daughter, Lucia, was preparing to follow a career working with horses, beginning her studies in South Africa. Luigi and I agreed that the solution to our dilemma was, for me to go to work as a live-in carer in the UK and earn some 'real' money. This might enable us to survive in Zimbabwe. Daniela by now had completed her time in America and had subsequently moved to the UK. With her already established over there it would really help me on this first trip to England. I was really looking forward to spending some time with her. So began preparations for me to travel to the UK, we bought my ticket on the 28 April 2006.

It was the year I turned fifty, a significant year in the Bible. Every fifty years the Jewish people celebrate the 'Year of Jubilee', as it is known.

For me it was going to be my year of new beginnings even though I did not realise it at the time.

.   *Leviticus 25 verse 10.*

"You shall thus consecrate the fiftieth year and proclaim a release through the land to all its inhabitants. It shall be a jubilee for you, and each of you shall return to his own property, and each of <u>you shall return to his family</u>" emphasis added.

The Ryrie Study Bible page 198

"JUBILEE: from and the restoration of man's lost inheritance, are proclaimed through Christ." It is as antitypically fulfilled in 'the acceptable year of the Lord,' this limited period of gospel grace in which deliverances from sin and death, and the restoration of man's lost inheritance, are proclaimed through Christ."

Fausset's Bible Dictionary Zondervan 1949 page 402

As this 50th year continued to unfold it revealed Father God's love to me and set me up for the amazing events that had been set in motion during this year.

An event of great significance to occur in this year of Jubilee, was the birth of my first grandson, he the son of my first born! This baby was born on my 50th birthday. I had no idea what events were being set in motion as a result of his birth.

Prior to us leaving Zimbabwe in 2006, I was visiting a dear friend, Cherry, whom I had known for a good number of years. We had a special friendship because we had both suffered much emotional trauma and we had found the Lord who heals. We connected in such a spiritual way a truly rare thing. It was to this friend that I had spoken about my first son, because I knew that she would understand my pain, and keep my secret.

Her words to me that day shocked me, she said, "Alison it is time for you to start looking for your son". These words seemed cruel; how could I ever face my son? My shameful secret still haunted me. I was emotionally incapable of doing this thing that Cherry was calling me to.

Soon after this event I was to travel to London. I arrived at Heathrow on the Saturday, where my daughter Daniela met me at the airport. My amazing Year of Jubilee began when I heard Daniela say, "Mom I never thought you would come and visit me!" All the years of her feeling rejection and not wanted or loved by me began to be healed.

The next morning Daniela taught me how to use the London public transport and, on the Monday, just for practice, I travelled on the Tube with her to work. It was like a dream; here I was in civilisation, just a few days before in a small village of Banket, Zimbabwe where donkey carts were the normal mode of transport for most of the rural population.

It was not easy for me to get a job in England. In the past, our lives revolved around following the direction of our Lord. As always, Father God has a plan for us, but that plan does not always work out the way we think it should. It still also true this time, but the plan was even more complex than I could imagine. I spent a good deal of time with my precious daughter. I would take a Tube into the centre of London, sometimes meet her for lunch, or just meet her to accompany her home on the Tube. I would prepare a meal, or we would go shopping together for food. Slowly she seemed to realise that I really did love her. It was truly a work of God!

I finally managed to get a job and was sent to take care of an elderly lady with terminal cancer. I lived in her house with her daughter and cared for this precious lady. I had time on my own and my journal evidenced some very special moments in my quiet time. Just days before I was due to return to Zimbabwe, this lovely lady passed away, in her own home with her daughter by her side.

On my return home I found Luigi had a surprise trip planned for us. We were to visit Inyanga, a mountainous beauty spot in the Eastern Highlands of Zimbabwe. This was to be my fiftieth birthday treat. It was also going to be a time for us to consider how we were going to continue.

Inyanga had always been my special place where I felt close to Father God. It is a beautiful, forested woodlands area with many trickling streams and thundering waterfalls. Luigi could not have chosen a better place to celebrate this special birthday. Lucia had accompanied us, with a dear friend of hers whom she had known since she was very young. It was our last time to visit this special place; for it was at this point we began to consider the possibility of leaving Zimbabwe. We had always thought that we would never leave Zimbabwe, it was radical for us even to be considering it. Not a decision we would be making in any kind of hurry.

Lucia was to leave Zimbabwe first; she went to South Africa to begin her Equestrian Studies. Lucia was our last child to leave home this would leave Luigi and I alone. We had a very large house that had served us well whilst we had all our family around us, but now it was just empty and quiet. We were grieving and not in a good place to make any kind of major decision.

Luigi had built a cottage on the property to house my mother and father who had lived with us for about ten years. Due to the unstable political climate and an economy that had been bankrupted, my parents had relocated to South Africa. We decided to move into the cottage and Luigi's brother and his family moved into the main house. To some degree, this helped to ease our loss over the children moving away.

With family and laughter around us again, we relaxed a bit and enjoyed the new situation. But the conditions in the country grew worse every day. No longer could we rely on having electricity in the house or water in our taps. The shops were empty, rows and rows of the same item, but no bread to be found. It became a real walk of faith just to have daily food to eat. But Father God was faithful, and our daily needs were always met. As we sat night after night by candlelight, we contemplated our situation. We were unable to phone or email any of our children because nothing was working. Inflation was rampant. Million-dollar banknotes were being printed, but you could buy very little with them.

We decided that it would be good to go and visit Giancarlo and his wife Natalie in America. But how could we do this in our current situation? We came up with a plan. Luigi had been asked to accompany Natalie's grandfather from Zimbabwe to America, her family offered to sponsor his ticket. I would return to England and resume work as a live-in carer. This would enable me to purchase a ticket and fly to America and meet Luigi there. By this time Lucia had completed her course in South Africa and had decided to further her equestrian studies in England.

And so, Lucia and I would travel together to the UK. This would enable me to see Lucia settled into her new situation, as well as to visit Daniela regularly. This time I managed to get work quickly. I remained at this job until it was time for me to fly to America.

At the airport in Atlanta, I met up with Luigi who had arrived there first. Giancarlo and Natalie had met him prior to my arrival. It came as a shock to me when I found Luigi very uncommunicative and withdrawn. I had never seen him like this before; he was unable to talk about what was troubling him.

It happened that we were scheduled to have a ten-day holiday at St George Island on the Gulf of Mexico near to Apalachicola in Florida. After we had arrived at this beautiful island and settled into our accommodation, Luigi was finally able to speak. He said, "I just can't go back there!" He broke down and we talked for a long time. He told me how bad it had been for him all on his own, and how things had just continued to deteriorate. We had been involved with a ministry whose mandate had been to care for widows and orphans in the town of Chinhoyi. The final straw for Luigi had been over some mosquito nets. A church in England that supported the ministry had sent the nets. The Zimbabwe Customs had impounded the mosquito nets and were demanding an exorbitant amount of money for them to be released.

Luigi had been tasked with the job of retrieving the nets from customs; it never happened. He was so angry for those orphans who could have benefitted from those mosquito nets.

We finally made the decision to leave Zimbabwe. Talking with Giancarlo and Natalie it seemed that I could possibly get a job as a nurse in America. This could be our ticket out of our situation. Of course, nothing ever works out as we initially imagine. We decided to begin our move to the USA by relocating to England first. And so, in January of 2008 I moved to the UK and began this new chapter in our lives, once again working as a live-in carer. We had left Zimbabwe with only our, suitcases. Luigi remained behind to settle things up; he arrived in the April of that year. And so, we began our new life. I had put in a lot of hard work and study trying to equip myself to work in America, but it never came to fruition. I was unable to get my registration to nurse in the USA approved.

It did, however, enable me to register as a nurse in England, and subsequently I served for many years as a nurse in England.

THE SEARCH BEGINS

Back in 2006, my 'Jubilee Year,' Father God began to fulfil His 'Jubilee' promise to me! In a faraway place a young couple were expecting a baby. It was my firstborn son and his wife. After the birth of their son, they realised it was time to try and find me. Their motivation was simple, to let me know that my son was in a good place. It never ceases to amaze me how incredible our God is. He chose this exact moment in time for the search to begin, it was not some random event, but all part of His plan for us.

Caleb John Daines was born at Constantiaberg Hospital in Cape Town on the exact day of my own 50th Birthday. All would be revealed as this incredible story continued to unfold.

In their search for me, the first thing they required was my son's original birth certificate, which would reveal my identity. It so happened that their neighbour, Betty, had also emigrated from Zimbabwe to South Africa. Prior to leaving Zimbabwe she had worked at the Director Generals office in Bulawayo. Betty was delighted to be of service, and it was Betty who arranged for the certificate to be found. It was at this point that the first difficulty immerged. The Authority would not release the birth certificate without written permission from my son's adopted mother.

His mother did not believe it was a good idea for them to try and find me; she was worried I would reject him and cause him untold pain. Then finally in 2007, whilst his mother was visiting the family in Cape Town she finally agreed.

They prepared two letters, one from his mother, giving her permission for any information regarding her son's biological parent to be released to her son. The second letter was from my son; he was asking for any information they could supply to enable him to contact his biological parents. He wrote in this letter,

"Although I have been blessed with two wonderful adoptive parents, I believe it would be good for my natural parents to know that I am doing well and am happy in life. Any information received will be treated with the utmost discretion and any attempts at making contact will be done discretely, realising the sensitive nature of adoption."

These letters were sent off on the 19th of January 2007, the authorities were now in a position to release his first birth certificate with my details on it.

The next hurdle would be, how to collect the birth certificate. The certificate was in Bulawayo, Zimbabwe. My son was a pastor of a church in Lakeside, Cape Town. His church hosted many bible students whilst they attended a local Bible School in nearby Muizenberg. One of those students was Lucy; she had attained a degree in Theology. After her graduation Lucy had returned to Zimbabwe to minister in Bulawayo. It was Lucy who was contacted. By co-incidence, Lucy was sitting in an Internet Café, across the road from the Director Generals Office. Whilst checking her emails she came across an email asking for her help. Her Pastor in Cape Town was asking her to collect his biological birth certificate from the Director Generals Office. Lucy was fully aware that her Pastor was searching for his biological mother, and how important this birth certificate was!

Lucy stopped what she was doing and left the café to go and collect the certificate. She soon realised there had been an administration error. She had been given the Adoptive Birth Certificate, not the original version that contained his birth parent's details. By quick thinking on her part, Lucy managed to get the problem resolved and left the office holding the original Birth Certificate in her hands.

That evening it was passed onto a friend who took it to Johannesburg the next day. It was then passed to another friend who was travelling down to Cape Town. Just two days later it was hand-delivered to their door. UK Royal Mail could not have delivered it faster.

The birth certificate revealed my name, Alison Patricia Walker, my father's name, John Robert Walker, and an address, 20 Camberley Road, Ashdown Park, Salisbury. Betty, the faithful neighbour, helped in every way that she could. Her garage in Cape Town was filled with old Zimbabwean telephone directories. She spent many hours looking through the directories trying to find us. She even enlisted another friend who lived in Zimbabwe to see what she could turn up. Neither of them had any success as, by this time, my mom and dad were living in a town called Springs, South Africa. Luigi and I were currently living in Banket, Zimbabwe.

Next, they turned to social media sites, Google, Facebook, Twitter and of course ancestry web sites, but found nothing. The address on the Birth Certificate suggested that I might have attended a girl's high school called Mabelreign Girls High. This was in fact true, but they could find no details of my having been there. Yet another dead end.

Another avenue they explored was the South African Drivers Licensing Department. They located my father, but the only information that this department could furnish was several speeding fines dad had collected along the way. We all had a little chuckle about this, as dad was known to be a bit heavy on the pedal.

Betty continued to search, this time in a South African publication called 'YOU Magazine'. One section of particular interest was called, 'Desperately Seeking'. This section was devoted to readers who were trying to find people with whom they had lost contact. Finally, in the February of 2009 Betty hit 'pay dirt' (a term used by prospectors who found gold). She found this notice:

"Seeking my biological mother. I was born on 28 August 1973 at Lady Rodwell Hospital, Bulawayo"
....
followed by an email address.

YOU Magazine- Desperately Seeking Column.
Pages 48,49

The Lady Rodwell Hospital! The same Hospital where my son was born, only one day after the girl who had placed the advert. Betty suspected that this girl's mother must have been at the hospital at the same time as I was! Betty ran over to my son's house with her find. Everyone was very excited at this breakthrough.

Finally, a real possibility had been unearthed. My son contacted the girl, who was living in Australia. She had indeed been re-united with her own birth mother and advised my son to contact Sandra her mother who was now living in Kempton Park, Johannesburg, South Africa. Sandra was the same girl with whom I had flown back to Salisbury all those years ago, after we had both given up our babies for adoption.

All this happened within days of Betty spotting the 'YOU magazine" advert. Sandra offered to put an advert into the 'YOU Magazine' on my son's behalf. As a buffer, she would say she was looking for a friend in case I did not want to be found. Sandra's advert read:

"Seeking Alison Patricia Walker who lived in Ashdown Park, Harare, in the 70's. We spent a couple of months together in 1973 in Bulawayo. Contact Sandra on" .... followed by her phone numbers and an email address.

This advert was posted in the April of 2010. Six weeks later, my dear friend Cherry saw it. This too was amazing as she was really the only one who knew about my son and was aware of all the details. The 'YOU Magazine' is very local to southern Africa and could not have been purchased in the UK where I was living by this time. On that Sunday Cherry had received some tragic news and, to take her mind off it, had purchased a copy of 'YOU Magazine'. She turned her attention to the 'Desperately Seeking' page; she was always hoping to catch up with people whom she had known. When she saw Sandy's advert, she knew straight away what it was all about. She was excited but also in a panic as she knew how carefully this secret had been kept over the years. Her first problem was that she did not have a phone number for me in England, so she emailed me and asked me, as casually as she could, for my phone numbers.

My friend Cherry.

The following morning Cherry called the phone number from the 'YOU Magazine' advert to contact Sandy in Kempton Park. She spent some time talking with Sandy over the phone that morning and voiced her concern about what she needed to do.

Sandra's response was *"Alison has a right to know"*. This settled all her concerns, Cherry realised that it was Father God at work on my behalf. Sandra was able to supply my son's name; Kevin John Daines, and that he lived in Cape Town. She gave Cherry his phone number. Sandra had come to faith and told Cherry that she would be praying. For us all, and for the best outcome. "Please could you keep me in the loop," was her only request.

That same evening Kevin phoned Cherry in Harare; Sandra had relayed Cherry's information to him. They talked for a long time, Cherry telling him everything that he wanted to know about Luigi and I and our family. She later told me he seemed tentative even anxious, somehow calm but nervous at the same time. Cherry told Kevin that she would call me the next morning as by this time I had already emailed her my phone number.

I was still in bed when Cherry rang in the morning, as I was due to work a night shift. To make this call Cherry had to summon all her courage. She too was very excited, but at the same time worried about my reaction after so many years of keeping this secret.

After the usual pleasantries, Cherry blurted out: *"Alison your son is looking for you."* There was silence on the line, I could only cry. There were no words to describe how immensely overjoyed I was to hear those words. When the conversation started again, I wanted to know everything that Cherry new. When she told me that Kevin was a Baptist Pastor, we just burst out into the most joyous laughter. He was serving the Lord; never in my wildest dreams did I imagine that. I had given him to the Lord as Hannah had given Samuel to God when he was just a very small boy. Now he was serving God, a mighty man of God indeed.

As soon as this call was ended, I called Luigi, who was at work. His main concern was our three children; they had never been told about my past. We needed to go forward with great care.

When Luigi came home from work, we talked. By this time, he had already come to realise that this was from God. We agreed we would tell our children the following weekend. Daniela was contacted in London. She was so intrigued that we wanted to see her in person, and just desperate for us to tell her what it was all about. She arrived quite early on the Saturday morning, so curious to know what was happening.

We told her the main details but then decided it would be better to go out to lunch at a local pub. I still remember the meals we eat that day, a speciality of this particular pub. It was Hot Pot Stew in a single ceramic pot for each of us. It was so hot it could have burnt our mouths if we had not been talking so much. Daniela wanted to know absolutely everything; she just kept pounding me with her questions. It was so wonderful to speak it all out loud, our relationship deepened as I answered her questions honestly and openly. Daniela was overjoyed to find she had another brother.

We told Lucia that evening when she came home from work. Her initial response was "That's really cool; I have another brother." It took her some years to really embrace Kevin as her other brother.

The next sibling to be told was Giancarlo who lived in America. It was our custom to call via Skype on a Sunday evening. That Sunday was no different. When Giancarlo called, Luigi handed the computer over to me, but we were having great difficulty with the connection due to the heavy thunderstorm on our side. Giancarlo realised there was something very important that I was trying to say but could not hear me due to the bad connection. Just at this point our nephew, who was staying with us at the time, came into the room. We could not tell him anything until all our children had been told. I took my phone and went out into the pouring rain with my umbrella to call Giancarlo. The rain pelted down over me, and my tears flowed as I told him about my incredible news. He just kept saying, "Mom it's okay, I love you it's okay". This was the son who had always wished that he had a brother; I was at last able to tell him the truth.

The next people I wanted to tell were my mother and father who were living in South Africa at this point. My dad was already 83 years old, and mom was 76 years old. I knew it would be a shock, but I also knew that the news would bring them much joy.

In the meantime, Cherry was in email contact with Kevin and was filling him in with as much information about us as she was able. Kevin told Cherry at the end of his first email,

"I am really excited about what is happening and hope it will be a great blessing for me and Alison to meet each other and whoever else may surface. How do you think we should go forward from here?"

"I better get back to work, I'll chat to you later."

When Kevin and Cherry realised the enormity of what was happening, they were both unable to work or even focus on anything else.

Our first meeting was scheduled via email. I desperately needed Kevin's forgiveness for abandoning him. I poured out my heart to him and he responded very graciously. Then he had a list of questions; he wanted to know about his roots. We carried on just trying to get to know each other via the emails, but Kevin found this difficult as it took so much time to write it all down Here are some extracts from that first email that I wrote.

"Dear Kevin,

How do I begin? The longing of a lifetime is coming to pass. Since Cherry phoned this morning, I have been dysfunctional, just allowing the memories to roll, feeling the emotions and trying to imagine where this will take us.

I have read the emails between you all, just to know that life has been so good to you is a comfort. I never really thought I could know; I had just turned 17 when you were born. I was alone in Bulawayo. I knew I was ill equipped to take proper care of you, and to walk away from you meant a part of me had to die. The only way I could do that was to lock it up inside and trust the people whom I left you with. My Aunt who lived in Bulawayo said she believed that she knew where you went and that she had seen you I just knew deep down that if I saw you, I could not walk away again. So, I never tried, I am sorry, please forgive me."

It was also in my first email to Kevin that I was able to tell him as much as I could about his biological father; his name, and what he had done for a living, as well as his love of fishing. It turned out to be quite easy to locate Peter. Kevin's wife Michelle discovered that Peter had won a fishing trophy in a competition for the printing trade. Peter was living in

129

Midrand, South Africa. Kevin called Peter who received him well and they began to get to know each other. Peter had two daughters, so Kevin and Michelle and the family travelled to Midrand to meet them all.

Lucia arranged an email with photos of all of us so that Kevin could have his first sight of us. I remember the night I opened Kevin's email and there was the first photo of him. I just sat there and looked and looked. There was never a shadow of doubt that he was mine. I kept going back to it again and again, I could not get enough of seeing him. I still find myself doing it, even now many years later.

I received an email from Kevin telling me of his reunion with his biological father.

On the 25 May, 2010 I recorded in my daily journal the following:

'Today I must face up to my own sin and depravity. The truth that I have kept in a box, to feel better about myself, to make Peter out to be the villain. Last night when I read Kevin's email about Peter. I had to see that I had never given Peter even a whisper of a chance. Peter made me feel so cheap and dirty, he made me feel so ashamed because I gave into him so easily.

I wanted to wait for that one special man that You had chosen for me. Then I go and give it all away to Peter and he just wiped his feet on me. Made me hate myself for being so weak and letting him do it. I have always thought about "what if" and I made his drinking and womanising a reason to justify giving Kevin up for adoption. So, I could somehow feel better about myself."

The entry continued until I came to a place of truth within myself. To a place where I really began to see the truth of what I had. I had Luigi who has brought out the best in me. I had not yet realised that Luigi and I had been destined for each other. I also saw that Peter was not this villain that I had built in my own mind but was a good family man who really loved his wife and children. The final part of this entry was a key place for me in my continuing journey to wholeness.

'So, You took my soiled filthy garments and gave me beauty and wholeness. Wow, Wow, and Wow again. I will be forever grateful, the enemy meant it for evil, but You have redeemed it all. I choose to forgive Peter, today I choose to forgive myself because You have forgiven me, Amen!'

I also had a burning desire to tell Kevin's adoptive mother how grateful I was to her. So, I asked Kevin if he would give me his mother's physical address. He was reluctant at first; he knew his mother well, having taken care of her for a long time after his father had passed away and was afraid, I might upset her. I finally managed to persuade him that all I wanted to do was to honour her for all the years of being his mother. To thank her and reassure her that she would always be Kevin's mother. Here is a small exert from that letter.

"Dear Lolly,

I have thought much about what I want to say in this letter and my overwhelming thought is the biggest thank you that you could ever imagine. To thank you for being his mother when I could not, to thank you for loving him and giving your life to raising him. Kevin obviously loved his father very much and told me how your prayers carried him through that difficult time in his life after Billy died. He is a real credit to you and your husband, who must be watching from heaven with pride. Our Father God is so amazing and as ever His timing is perfect.

We are very excited to meet you when we come over in September"

"No words can really describe what this has all meant to me, I never deserved it, but by His Grace I have been given this wonderful joy, it really does not get much better than this.

So, thank you, thank you and thank you again" May the
Lord continue to bless you, Alison."

Kevin had been adopted into a family who at that point were living in Bulawayo. His new mother already had one son of her own but, after numerous premature births, had given up hope of having another baby. The couple had applied to adopt a child and had waited two years before that day came and they were told he was coming. He brought such joy and comfort to his new family, at last healing for all the pain they had suffered over the many babies they had lost. Some months later she would write to me to tell me these events here is an extract from that letter:

1 June 2010

"The Lord is truly great, and He always is there to work His miracles but in His own time, and His timing is perfect. When we had Darrell, we tried for years to have another child but to no avail we just had to pray and then in God's wisdom He gave us Kevin. What a joy he has been for us, he excelled in school and sport. He and Billy his father was very close and when he was small, he and his dad would go off fishing at the crack of dawn, and if they caught anything Kev would gut and descale them. YEAGH. Billy was a

man of good character, honest and a gentleman and always treated the boys equally and he loved them both dearly. He instilled in them the qualities and good traits they have today, and I am very proud of them both."

We were already using Skype to stay in touch with Giancarlo in America, and now we began to plan our first visual meeting with Kevin. He arranged to get a camera for his computer and then we made the date for our first Skype meeting. Kevin was also able to meet his new brother and sisters by this means. Even now it is difficult to describe how amazing it was to see him and talk to him. Slowly but surely the strangeness of if all began to diminish, and with each call we began to relax more in each other's company.

REUNITED

A family wedding was being planned; it was to become a big Family Reunion. The date for the wedding coincided with my mom and dad's sixtieth Wedding Anniversary and become a once in a lifetime event. It would coincide with our plan to move my mother and father to the UK. The main event of course was to be the wedding, so also included all of Luigi's family as well as some very special friends.

It was to this event that we were planning to introduce Kevin and his family to the entire family! Everyone coming knew all about the whole amazing story so there was much excitement building up in the various places around the world where our family had been scattered.

Lolly (Kevin's mother) and I made plans to meet one another the Sunday before the wedding. The venue was to be a resort south of Durban Natal called the Happy Wanderers, that was owned by a family member.

The wedding was scheduled for September of 2010. It was to be a truly Italian affair; the entire family were planning to gather. The owner of the resort had offered to accommodate all the guests at their resort as part of their contribution to the wedding expenses. This being the case it had been decided early in its planning to have the wedding to take place during the low season. This amazingly generous offer created a family celebration never to be forgotten by all who attended. It set the stage for the entire family to meet Kevin in a non-threatening environment with loads of space.

Some of the family began to assemble three weeks before the day of the wedding. One of them, the event's planner, would take responsibility of co-ordinating all the many details to be fitted together. Luigi and I were to follow planning to arrive two weeks prior to the week of the wedding.

Giancarlo, Natalie and their two boys Ethan and Noah came to the UK first from the States. This enabled us to travel together with them to South

Africa. The second stage of the journey was by far the longest part and our help with the little ones was needed. On arrival in Durban airport, Daniela met us with the news that my mom had suffered a stroke. She was in the Intensive Care of a hospital in Johannesburg. I was totally exhausted after a nearly 22-hour trip from London with two little people, I was having some difficulty in assimilating what was being said to me. I was in shock! I asked if we could go to the resort and get some rest before I would be able to decide the best course of action.

The following morning, I found myself up early. I was alone as everyone else was still asleep. In my journal I wrote:

'Crying for mom, I thought I had more time. I thought I was in heaven and had left the trials and sorrows of this world. But alas I am still here. But You my precious, awesome Father are with me. Thank You I am here and not in England. Thank You that they were with Stuart (my older brother) and not alone in Springs where they had been living) Thank You that dad was not alone when it happened.'

So that same day instead of being with the family in the final preparations, I was on a plane heading to Johannesburg. My brother Stuart met me at the Airport and while taking me to his home told me exactly what had occurred.

Mom and Dad, we knew, were not coping on their own. Dad was evidencing some early signs of Dementia. Mom had been trying to cope as best she could but as a result, she had not been managing her Diabetes well. Her Blood sugars had been running excessively high for some months according to her Specialist Doctor. This had resulted in extensive damage to some areas of her brain. We already had a plan in place to move them to the UK after the celebrations, but we had not realised how desperate their situation had become.

At the Hospital mom was in very capable hands, and it soon became evident that, once her blood sugars stabilised, she should make a good recovery. My dad was very happy to see me, as were my three brothers who lived in Johannesburg at that time. Everyone felt reassured as we gathered, and my arrival enabled us to be together and support one another.

It had been a good call to go to Johannesburg and be with my brothers, I knew that I was in the place where Father God wanted me to be.

Kevin and his family were due to arrive in Durban a week before the rest of the guests. It became evident that I would not be able to meet them at the airport on their arrival. I needed to remain in Johannesburg until my mother's condition was stabilised and she would be ready for discharge from the Hospital. As soon as the Specialist told us that she was ready for discharge I started trying to book my ticket back to Durban.

I could get a flight back on the same day as Kevin and his family, but the only one available was some time after they would have landed. It would be Luigi who would meet them, and Daniela would then take them to the Resort. Luigi would wait at the airport for my arrival, as the airport was some distance from the resort.

This poignant moment of my reunion with Kevin would now take place at The Happy Wanderers. My streams of emotions were so high I thought I would burst! I had imagined this moment so many times, playing it through my mind, and now it had all been displaced.

I found myself praying much to calm this storm. By nature, I am a very intense; my brothers called me the 'Drama Queen'. But Father God had it all in His hands. Luigi was by far the best one to be there at the airport. He embraced Kevin as a father would. He played sports with Caleb and Zoe and so their first moments with their new family where exactly what God had intended, warm loving and totally natural.

Finally, after an hour's drive by car we arrived at the Resort where we were meet face-to-face. I was taken to their apartment on the ground floor facing the majestic Indian Ocean, the waves rolling in constantly. This reflected the emotions that I was feeling, sometimes high and thunderous. At other points gentle and playing in the background.

The family came out onto their veranda, and we met at last face to face. I wanted to embrace him, just to love on him but I was unable to do this. It may have been the strangeness of it all. I think that it was my deep-seated feeling of unworthiness to be given this amazing gift. This embrace would come a few days later when we were able to celebrate his birthday together. Almost like the embrace I would have given him when he had been born, then taken away from me.

This new chapter in our lives was ushered in by a whole week of celebrations, just getting to know all the family who assembled in dribs and drabs over the course of that week. Giancarlo had been asked if he would conduct the wedding ceremony, but he was very nervous, so Kevin volunteered to help. And so, it came about that the two new brothers had this opportunity to work together on the wedding program, as Kevin was also a Marriage Officer in South Africa it all made perfect sense.

Even though Giancarlo had been to Bible School and his major was in Preaching, he really suffered from nerves when called upon to speak in public. Kevin on the other hand was a well-seasoned Pastor and was accustomed to speaking in public. My delight to see them working together on this assignment knew no bounds! Both Kevin and Giancarlo were devoted fathers, each with two small children, and they spent many happy hours on the beach with each other and their children, just getting to know each other.

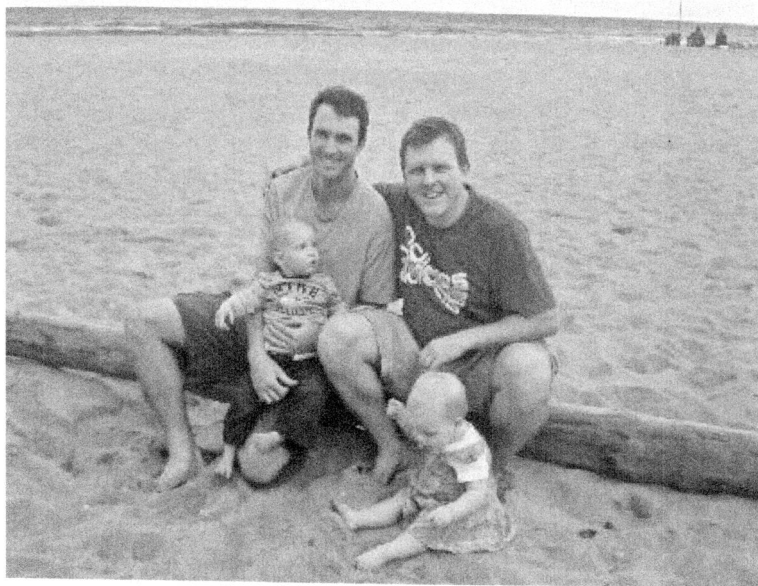

Giancarlo and Kevin on the beach together

This final week of preparations was amazing; I would refer to it as a little piece of heaven here on earth. The Italian part of the family is like an organic organism just bursting with life and vitality. Much laughter and nonsense going on while attending to the many details that had been planned for the celebrations. The table decorations were beautiful silver candlesticks that had been decorated with strings of crystals. So, the Italian's got busy stringing the beads, stringing each other and generally have a laugh while they were doing it.

Then there was the Ravioli to be made for 200 guests. My dear mother-in-law was the overseer to ensure we kept at work and the result was of an excellent standard. It was more of a military operation to achieve such an ambitious goal. But there was music and laughter to keep us all going, as well as many visits from other family members who were hoping for a little taste.

In all this nonsense and bravado Kevin, Michelle, Caleb and Zoe were included. They were welcomed into all the different apartment's, Caleb made friends and loved to visit his new 'cousins' wherever he might find them. Zoe and Noah, Kevin's youngest daughter and Giancarlo's youngest son were the babies, very popular with everyone.

Mom and dad had been flown down to Durban accompanied by one of their granddaughters. They had been billeted in a downstairs flat, where they could sit outside in the sea air and watch all that was going on around them. Our apartment was directly above theirs, so I was able to take care of them and ensure that mom's recovery continued. Dad escorted mom as she slowly began taking walks along the pathway in front of their flat. She began slowly regaining her strength. Two of my three brothers also joined us with their families. There was a lot of planning to be accomplished for this great move to the UK to succeed. My brothers agreed to take charge of all the logistics of the move.

Two days before the day of the wedding happened to be Kevin's birthday, I went to try and buy him a present and suddenly realised that I had no idea what he might like. A painful reminder for me of all the birthdays I had missed. On the morning of Kevin's birthday, I took Kevin into my arms and, just hugged him for the longest time. I felt like something that had been broken had finally been mended.

The Sunday before the wedding, Michelle's mom brought Lolly, Kevin's adoptive mother, to Happy Wanderers resort for the day to enable us to meet. What a happy day we had together Lolly and me.

We just talked and talked. She told me everything she could about her son whom she obviously loved a great deal, also about her life with Billy her husband. Lolly brought photos of Kevin as a baby and some as he grew up. We talked as we sat close to one another. Everyone and everything else excluded from this amazing encounter. We only had one day; it was almost like we knew we had to make the most of every moment we had together.

Although we continued to write after our amazing meeting, Lolly's health had not been good for a while and sometime later, she passed away. When Michelle contacted me to tell me that she had gone I was so grateful to have had this special day with this gracious lady who had been my son's mother.

Laura, Kevin and I, what an amazing day we had together.

The day of the wedding came; it was to be on the beach. The Marque' was beautifully decked with flowers; the tables inviting you to come in and dine in elegance. Chairs had been set out on the beach to the side of the Marque' garlanded in flowers. The backdrop that we gazed upon was the mighty

Indian Ocean with its waves relentlessly rolling onto the sandy beach. Everyone assembled, no shoes on because of the sandy beach, but all dressed beautifully. Kevin and Giancarlo managed their duties as if they had known each other all their lives. The party that night went on very late with much feasting, and dancing celebrating in true Italian style.

Mom and dad's sixtieth Wedding Anniversary was the day after the wedding. They had nearly all their children and grandchildren around them. Of course, they had been able to meet Kevin and his family. Their special anniversary was celebrated in style.

The days came when everyone started to leave the resort, many goodbye conversations and meals. We could not be sad it had been a truly awesome gathering with so much to celebrate. We already had a plan afoot for Kevin to visit us in England. He had a ministry trip at the planning stage, to go to Greece, so it was hoped he would be able to take some time out to visit with us.

There was another significant birth event that had taken place that we had discovered as we talked. Michelle, Kevin's wife, had been born at Addington Hospital in 1977. The very year I was doing my Midwifery training. So as soon as I returned to England, I took out the record of Mandatory Training, the evidence of my Midwifery Course. One of the requirements of my training was that I had to witness five births before I would be allowed to assist in the delivery of a baby.

Everything I did was recorded in this journal as part of the evidence of my training. It also had to be witnessed by a senior member of staff. There it was, in black and white, Michelle's mothers name, the Doctors name, date and a baby girl. Michelle was the very first baby I had witnessed being born! How can you not trust a God who is watching over every detail of your life, it had not 'just happened' it was not random but further confirmed what we already knew. The hand of God in our lives, Father God involved with us intimately, in the small things as well as the major events.

All the siblings and some of their children.

Kevin's Joins his Tribe

Once back in the UK we ran into a busy time, I was back at work, as was Luigi. We were preparing to receive my mom and dad; having decided the best room for mom and dad would be the one we had been using. Luigi and I needed to move into another room off the main building but still connected. It was smaller so some adaptations needed to be made.

Before we could commence the work, this room was needed to accommodate my friend Cherry and her husband. They would be in England for a short stay and wanted to spend a weekend with us. It was only going to be a one-night stop, but after all that had gone on before I was really looking forward to seeing Cherry. And to have a chance to share all the amazing things that had happened. They arrived as expected and, during one of the many conversations Cherry asked Luigi what he thought about it all, his reply reflects aptly what it had all meant for us. Here is what he said,

"If I hadn't believed in God before I certainly would now. Now I know there is a God!"

I asked Luigi recently,

"From when you first knew that Kevin would be coming back into our lives and to the present day. How have you been impacted?"

His reply was quite simple

" So blessed, overjoyed, and overwhelmed. I rejoice every day for Kevin being restored to us. What a blessing to us all, and I believe our family has been strengthened as he has become a part of us."

Mom and dad arrived in the October; our lives were instantly changed in every aspect. We found that they had both become quite frail and my father, who had always been very strong, was totally dependent on mom for his security. His dementia had worsened due to the many changes he had come through. Soon and with help we were able to make adaptations to our home and get them involved with a Bible Study Group as well as a Lunch Club. As a routine became more entrenched, we found that dad became more relaxed. Mom's health benefitted much from the better management of her diabetes.

At this point Lucia was also living with us so it was a full house. Kevin's plans to visit whilst on a ministry trip to Greece came to fruition. Although he would only be with us for a week, we were very excited for another opportunity to spend some time together. As a nurse my ROTA was set, I did not have any available Annual Leave remaining due to the trip to South Africa. I was disappointed to find I would miss some of the days that he would be with us. However, Luigi and Lucia arranged some wonderful sight-seeing trips on those days and could spend time with Kevin.

It was whilst touring the sights of Winchester that Lucia became very upset with Kevin. He was treating her like his little sister, giving her a hard time and generally being more affectionate than she was comfortable with.

As there had been so much going on in our lives, I had not picked up on the fact that Lucia had withdrawn into herself and from many of the things that were going on during the 'Family Reunion'. She was not happy about his arrival at all.

Lucia and I had a very close relationship over the years of Home Schooling, she felt betrayed by me. I had not confided in her about Kevin, and when he burst into her life, she was simple not ready to embrace him. She did not know him, and she did not want to get to know him. The other aspect of this was that she was afraid that if she told me the truth about how she was feeling I might reject her in favour of Kevin. Our relationship was too important for her to risk this. Most of the time at the wedding she had been able to hide because there was so much going on. She continued to hide how she was really feeling, guilty that she had not taken Kevin into her heart as everyone else had done.

Otherwise, Kevin's trip had been a success, we had more time just together to really begin to get to know each other. He was also able to get to know his grandparents a bit better. He was really kind to them in all his interactions with them. I made some tentative plans for me to go to Cape Town to visit with him in his home environment. And so sometime later I made my own trip to Cape Town. It was to be the best thing for me to do. I was away from work and all my family commitments. At last, we would be able to have the time to just visit with each other.

I was warmly welcomed into their home, and met Betty, their neighbour who had been so instrumental in finding me. I was able to interact with the children in their environment and simple be a small part of their lives, each step bringing us closer.

It set in motion a plan to try and see each other each year; Luigi would travel to Zimbabwe usually in January to see his family and especially his mother. He would never plan a trip without adding the extra leg to visit Cape Town and stay with Kevin and his family. He usually went alone, as I had limited Annual Leave, but always had a special time with them all.

Caleb and Zoe just loved their new Nonno (Italian version of Granddad).

We also had to plan for mom and dad's care if we went away together. As a result, we would travel on our own, one of us would remain behind to care for them. I visited Cape Town initially on my own, but as time went on Luigi and I have tried to make these trips together.

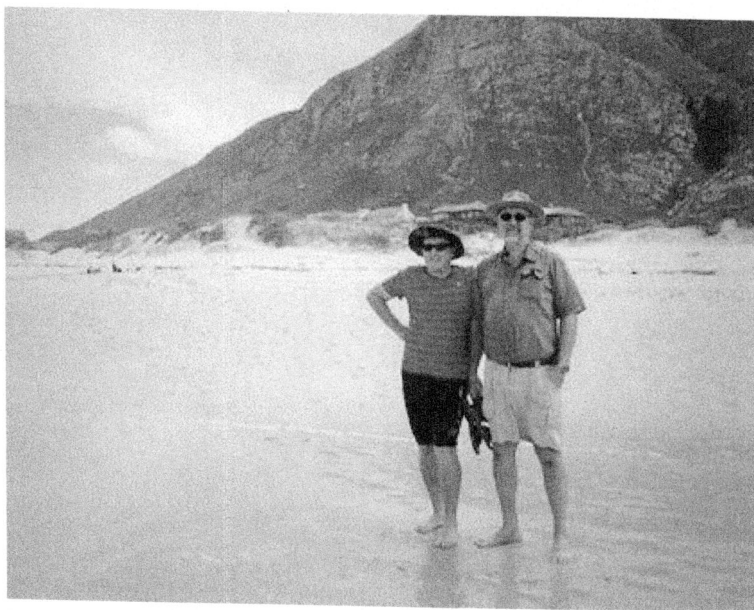

Luigi and Kevin, Cape Town beach.

Actually meeting Betty

Alison with Zoe and Michelle

The desire to bring Kevin into the family was very strong in me, and whilst taking with Kevin and Michelle and the rest of the family we began to plan another family reunion, this time just for our four children and their families. Kevin wanted to bring his family over to the UK for a holiday.

Giancarlo and Natalie also came on board with the idea. Three weeks in March 2011 was chosen. I began to plan how they could be accommodated, also how we could have another family time like the one that we had experienced in South Africa.

I managed to lease a farmhouse for two weeks. Kevin and his family, as well as Giancarlo and his family would stay in it together. Luigi bought a second-hand car; we already had another spare car, so that we were able to provide them with transport. We wanted them to have the freedom to come and go as they pleased.

This time was very precious, most evenings we would gather at The Barn, where we were living at the time, for dinner and shared some wonderful times of fellowship together.

It was Luigi's birthday in the mix, which we held at the local village hall. It was summer in England and the weather was lovely. Each day we were busy just trying to catch up on all the years we had missed.

The final event that I planned was a holiday down in Cornwall. I had found a family Fixed Caravan Park in Cornwall. It would be off-season, but the park had plenty of room for all of us to be accommodated. Each family had their own Fixed Caravan according to their needs. It was thus possible for our four children and their families to enjoy each other and their children to also meet their cousins again now a little older.

My brother Ian and his family joined us too, so it felt more like the family gathering I was hoping for. Added to this mom and dad could be included and have a holiday as well. They would share our Caravan and could still be involved in what was going on.

Both families arrived on the same day at different airports, so Luigi went to collect Giancarlo and his family, and I went to fetch Kevin and his family. Then back to The Barn. Followed by settling into the farmhouse. The farmhouse was rustic with a wood stove for heating and a country style kitchen where everything happened. Here I really began to enjoy all four of my grandchildren. It was such a joy to be with them, I loved to read them stories of an evening.

I was even able to stay over one night to enable the moms and dads to have a date night. Different activities were planned each day according to what the family wanted to achieve on their holiday.

I imagined that the trip to Cornwall would be the best part, but the lovely weather we had been enjoying broke and, it became cold, rainy and grey. We were confined to our Caravans a lot, and we had to keep the fires burning most of the time. My brother Ian and his family had joined us, and their presence added much to our enjoyment of this time together. We took mom and dad to Lands' End on one of the days, it was raining, and cold. We had all spent most of our lives in hot Africa, so the cold seemed very cold indeed. Kevin was so kind to his grandmother and gave up his jacket for her. She treasured this memory of her grandson.

It was Easter Weekend and Kevin and I planned to celebrate a 'Passover Meal' on the Friday evening. Once again, I enlisted the help of everyone to prepare the meal. Kevin planned the program and, we had a special time sat in my car, with the rain falling all around us. We used the CD player in the car to enable us to choose the music for the evening. We held the event in the Park's main restaurant, as there were few guests in the park at the time. It was a special evening of fellowship and fun, making of new memories together.

Lucia began to thaw a bit with Kevin and his family; she particularly enjoyed the Easter egg hunt on the Sunday morning with her niece and nephews. It helped that she had Ed her fiancé, had come with her. So, she was able to relax a bit and enjoy the time they had together.

Of course, all too soon we had to return to Hampshire, the time had come for us all to say goodbye.

Life is made up of memories. At the time we do not always consider how precious and valuable these memories are. I had missed all my son's growing up, and the memories and events that had made up his life to this point. It felt good to be making our own memories together.

There are two events that I consider really brought us round to becoming a family together. The first one came from Lucia; she came to realize that she did not really have a problem with Kevin, but that it was really with me. She wrote an email to Kevin as she felt that she needed to make right with him. I will quote some extracts from their emails:

"Dearest Kevin,

This may seem out of the blue and I guess it is, but I need to do this. I know we don't talk much and that I don't really know you. This is my own fault, and I would like to change that. I am so grateful to you for never giving up on Mom. When you found her, you set a part of her free that had been hiding for so very long. She delights in you and your family, and I really and very truthfully feel that she is better for it....

...However, I really struggled getting my head around it all. I never told mom, ... but I felt very betrayed by

her not ever telling us. Mom and I have always been close, even friends and I were hurt that she had never told me. I didn't want to hurt her feelings, so I pretended that I was as happy as the rest of the family. Unfortunately for you I think that because I did not express my feelings the hurt was all directed at you........... Because of these feelings I kept my distance from you and sadly from your beautiful family. For this I am truly sorry. I have struggled with this for some time now, uncertain of how I felt about you or your family.

I am sorry it has taken so many years, and I hope that one day we can be close. .... I hope that you will be able to forgive me, as I am very sorry...........please will you accept this offer of becoming my big brother.

Lucia."

Kevin's response to Lucia's heartfelt sorrow over how she had felt about him:

"Dear Lucia,

It's good to hear from you!..............................

It must have taken a lot to write this and could not have
been easy. I admire you for it, it shows what a deep person
you are. It is so good when people open up and honestly
speak to each other to share their thoughts and feelings.
Bursting into your world like I did must have been a shock
and something you did not ask for. So, I do sympathies with
how you must have felt and certainly don't hold anything
against you for it. I am so glad you have worked through it
and come out where you where you have.

We have been overwhelmed by the acceptance received by
all the family, and really did not expect it. Even from you,
there must be a lot of love in your heart, to forgive me,
because I did not feel what you were feeling towards me. I
have always enjoyed the times we have spent together-
Happy Wanderers and our trip to the UK and particularly
the fishing trip at Lands' End.

I hope mom's silence never comes between your relationship
with her. She loves you dearly and would not want that.
She always talks with such love, affection and appreciation

for you. I encourage you to tell her what you have been working through when you feel ready.

I don't think you need to apologize for your feelings, but I gladly accept it, forgive you and take up your offer of being your big brother!

We love you and Ed! Keep well

Kevin"

This was a huge breakthrough in their relationship and two years later Kevin and Giancarlo officiated at Lucia and Ed's wedding. We were all together again; with each encounter our family became more integrated and whole.

I asked Lucia if Kevin's arrival had changed her. This was her response.

"I'm not sure really, I guess I have learnt that even though I struggled with the idea of a new family member, things have still worked out beautifully. I've learnt that it was ok for me to feel hurt and confused, so long as I never let that determine how I would respond. In the end I realised this; I was able

to let go of negative feelings and begin to embrace my new family members"

The other significant event to take place was Luigi's decision to include Kevin in his Will as one of his children. I asked him to tell me what his thought process that led his to the place of including Kevin into his will. His reply was,

"It was just so simple for me to add Kevin to my Will as he is my son, and he is such a part of us, how could he not be included in my Will."

Luigi first spoke to Giancarlo, Daniela and Lucia to get their responses and feedback. He wanted them to know in advance so that there would not be any surprises that might cause a problem.

Giancarlo's response
"This is a no brainer for me as Kevin is one of the siblings so wouldn't he be included in the Will. I am glad Papa and Mom rectified this formality quickly"

Daniela's response
"Well of course he should be included in the Will! He's, our brother. Thank you for taking care of that and making it official"

Lucia's response

"I was surprised initially, but not because I didn't want Kevin to be included, more that Papa and mom felt they needed to ask our permission. I had

assumed it was already the case as he was now part of our family"

They had all agreed that Kevin is indeed part of our tribe, and this legal inclusion was simple an evidence of what had already taken place.

Kevin's response, "When I was told of my inclusion in papa's Will I was filled with mixed emotions. It was such a massive gesture in terms of officially making me part of the family that was so special to me, and I was very thankful for this. But I was concerned that it might not be well received by my siblings which I did not want. I remain deeply touched by this gesture."

Indeed, a journey to wholeness for me, as well as my family. My brother Ian asked me the question, after reading my story "So Alison are you whole now?"

On reflection I believe that wholeness is an ongoing process. Father God is never finished with us, thank goodness. We do still fall, but he never let's go of us and never gives up on us. Praise His wonderful name HALLELUJAH!!

EPILOGUE

Our lives continue, we endeavour to make them intersect as often as possible. Covid 19 and lockdowns have made this a challenge, but we have found ways. As individuals our children communicate with each other. We as a family shared a meal over Zoom and continue to share one another's lives with the help of WhatsApp.

Luigi gave me these words of wisdom:

"In the light of all the amazing things God has done I now have a much greater appreciation of how much our FATHER loves us. We have been blessed by an amazing miracle that has been life changing. God has shown us His faithfulness, goodness, grace and above all HIS love. I hope that these blessings can shine brightly through this book, that people might know that GOD is real."

Few words from Giancarlo:

"It has been truly amazing to see God bring this incredible miracle about. I put it on a par with the miracle of someone being raised from the dead. It has affected me personally in my own faith. I have seen with my own eyes real hard undeniable proof that God is real! The mathematical odds are on the impossible level of this happening. Where mom was at the birth of Kevin's wife. Kevin started to look for mom on her 50th birthday, her year of jubilee. His firstborn son was born, exactly on moms' birthday!!!! So, yes it has affected me hugely, in a positive way. I share this testimony of God's amazing love where-ever I can.

Since meeting Kevin my life has been greatly enriched! I had always longed for a brother growing up. That longing has been fulfilled. Not just with another member being added to our tribe. But with a big brother everyone wished for. One who is wise, level-headed strong and always looking out for you. I truly look up to Kevin as he inspires me to live well.

I think of how proud I am of the humanitarian work Kevin and Michelle have been doing through his church during this pandemic. It just shows what a precious gift of life mom gave by choosing adoption rather than abortion. God is good always and is with us through our darkest hours."

Some words from Daniela:

"There is no doubting that God's handiwork can be seen in the restoration that has happened between mum and Kevin, all the fine detail that just blows me away every time. How powerful prayer is. My initial reaction was anger at the lies, which was short lived, and then replaced with sheer excitement to meet a long-lost brother. Sad, we had missed out on a childhood together, but glad to be reunited. Kevin, Michelle, Caleb and Zoe have become such an intrinsic part of the family now, it is hard to imagine them not being there, as if they have always been part of our family. Whenever I talk about my family, I always talk about my two brothers and one sister with great pride. I feel so incredibly blessed to be part of this crazy crew!"

Some words from Lucia:

"I think that it is great that after so many years of loss and grief mom has finally been able to find peace. Its great having a new family member. I wish we lived closer so we could spend more time together. I feel privileged to be a part of something I could never have imagined for myself.

The incredible circumstances that led to Kevin and mom finding each other always gives me a warm feeling."

And finally, a few words from Kevin himself:

"Bringing me home to my family has given me a fresh appreciation of the goodness of God in opening the door to find one another... that He cares so much about us to do such a thing for us. This became very real to me and personal. God loves us and takes care of us even in the finer details of life. The whole thing was beyond coincidence and truly a work of God, that God would do this for us is amazing and touched me deeply.

My initial response to finding you was unbelievable, even surreal. After such a long wait, the uncertainty of who my biological mother was, was over. But naturally you were still very much stranger to me. There was no understanding of who you are, no relationship, no history, no memories. The initial emails, then Skype calls were helpful to start the process of getting to know each other. But it was the family reunion that was incredible!

To get to meet everyone and spend extended meaningful time together as a family. My first trip to the UK did wonders to experience you in your environment and gave me a much better feel for your world. The next trip to the UK also did wonders to be together and make memories for me and Michelle and the kids. It was important for me that my family get to know our new family along with me. On one occasion Luigi, Giancarlo and myself attended a church men's meeting in Winchester, we eat curry. At this event, Luigi introduced me to others as his firstborn son. This was so incredibly profound to me! I felt I did not deserve to be introduced as such and was concerned Giancarlo might feel threatened or his place usurped. At some point, I raised my concern to you, but you assured me that Giancarlo always wanted an older brother and was quite secure in his place in the family and his relationship with his father Luigi. This gave me peace and I have seen this over the years. The visits by you and Luigi were particularly significant to me. I felt that you guys were making a real effort to connect and get to know us in our environment and community. That you went the extra mile was very important to me. All this served to grow our confidence and place in the family and our relationship. The acceptance by you, Luigi, my siblings and even Da Familia and Walkers has been outstanding, and beyond what we ever dared to imagine. This has all served to make us feel secure and part of the family.

"It is hard to describe what having you all in our lives has meant to us. From not really having a family anymore with my dad and mom's passing, God has put us back into a family. You have made every effort to integrate us into the family and we are so thankful for this."

Psalm 68: 4-6. Describes how we feel:

4.   *Sing to God, sing in praise of his name,*

Extol him who rides on the clouds, Rejoice before him--his name is the LORD.

5.   *A father of the fatherless, a defender of widows, is God in His holy dwelling.*

6.   *God sets the lonely in families,*

he leads out the prisoners with singing.

Taken from the New International Version.

The Lord has blessed us as a family. We do not know what the future holds, but that God holds the future. What he has done in terms of His goodness and kindness gives us so much to look forward to.

The Way of Salvation

This story would not be complete unless I show you my reader the way of salvation. It begins with.

John 3:16,

"For God so loved the world that He gave His only begotten Son, that whoever believes in Him should not perish, but have eternal life."

The Ryrie Study Bible page 1604

This is a very clear promise from our loving Heavenly Father.

Romans 5:8,

"But God demonstrates His own love toward us, in that while we were yet sinners, by the fact that while we were yet still sinners, Christ died for us."

The Ryrie Study Bible, page 1708.

This verse clearly tells us that it is while we are still sinners! In other words, it is not when we get our lives together and stop all our sinning. But while we are still sinning that He proves His love for us by dying for us.

2 Corinthians 5:21

"He made Him who knew no sin to be sin on our behalf, that we might become the righteousness of God in Him."

The Ryrie Study Bible, page 1759

This is truly an amazing statement from the heart of God. That Father God put all our sin and guilt upon the Christ, the only sinless Son of God. A gift so incredible! And we can receive it by His goodness towards us.

1 Timothy 2:5,6.

"For there is one God, and one mediator also between God and men, the man Christ Jesus who gave Himself as a ransom for all, the testimony borne at the right and proper time."

The Ryrie Study Bible, page 1817

When we consider what a mediator does, we see that it was Jesus is our mediator. He made it possible for the ransom to be paid in full, that we may go free.

The final scripture I would like to share with you is,

1 Peter 3:18

"For Christ also died for sins once for all, the just for the unjust, in order that He might bring us to God, having put to death in the flesh, but made alive in the spirit;"

The Ryrie Study Bible, page 1869

So, His death for our sins only took place once, yet it covers all of history and every person who has ever been born! Why? Because Jesus Christ is the only sinless human to have ever lived on earth, and He was the only one who qualified to take away such great multitudes upon multitudes of sins.

So how do I get this amazing gift I hear you asking? It is so simple, all you must do is ask, then believe you have received it. I will give you a short prayer you can use to help you to receive this most amazing gift of freedom from guilt and sin.

Dearest Lord Jesus,

Please forgive my sins which are many.

I believe that you died upon that cross, to become my mediator. Please take away my guilt and sin.

I ask you to bring me to your Father, that I can begin my new relationship with Him. Thank you for coming into my life.

Amen

It is as simple as that, as you read in this book it was when I became a part of a Bible believing Church that my new life in Him really began. If you have prayed that prayer it has now begun. Now would be a good time to start to read His love letter to you, His Word the Bible. Seek out other believers who will be delighted to help you, and of course the Angels in heaven are all rejoicing over another sinner coming home.

BIBLIOGRAPHY

Caldwell Ryrie Charles, Th.D., Ph.D. (1978). *The Ryrie Study Bible*. Chicago: Moody Press. P. 1706, 1606, 1866, 1454, 928, 1745, 941, 1712, 1857, 1744, 1713, 198, 1604, 1708, 1759, 1817, 1869.

Fausset A.R. (1949). *Fausset's Bible Dictionary*. USA: Zondervan. P. 402.

Lindsey Hal (1970). *The Late Great Planet Earth* USA: Zondervan. P. 186-188.

New International Version (NIV), Biblica (formerly International Bible Society (OT,1978, NT1973) (Revised 1978, 2011) Biblica (worldwide) Zondervan (US), Hodder & Stoughton.

You Magazine Article (1 April 2010). Desperately Seeking column. South Africa: You Magazine Publishers. P. 48,49.

Williams Margery (1997). Rainbows through Clouds. 2nd ed. Farnham: A3 Design &Print Ltd Farnham. P.1.

Acknowledgements

A great big thank you to my children who have given me some much-needed practical advice. Kevin and Michelle for persevering through those years to find me. Giancarlo and Natalie for enabling me to publish with their financial support. Daniela for her creative artwork in the design of the cover. Lucia for being willing to tell her mother that the first draft was really rubbish, but not leaving me there but continuing to work alongside me till it became a readable book.

My dear friend Cherry, who had the courage to put her own feelings and fears aside to unite me with my son. Where would this have gone without you?

My dear friend Helga, who persevered through editing the first draft. Getting my sentence structure sorted out as well as keeping me accurate.

I have altered some names to protect the individuals' privacy.

Printed in Great Britain
by Amazon